THE A
BRING
BOYS:

C000112871

Positive Parenting Strategies to Raise Worry-Free and Strong Sons in a World of Anxiety

Aurora Morris

© Copyright 2020 - All rights reserved.

The content contained within this book may not be reproduced, duplicated or transmitted without direct written permission from the author or the publisher.

Under no circumstances will any blame or legal responsibility be held against the publisher, or author, for any damages, reparation, or monetary loss due to the information contained within this book. Either directly or indirectly.

Legal Notice:

This book is copyright protected. This book is only for personal use. You cannot amend, distribute, sell, use, quote or paraphrase any part, or the content within this book, without the consent of the author or publisher.

Disclaimer Notice:

Please note the information contained within this document is for educational and entertainment purposes only. All effort has been executed to present accurate, up to date, and reliable, complete information. No warranties of any kind are declared or implied. Readers acknowledge that the author is not engaging in the rendering of legal, financial, medical or professional advice. The content within this book has been derived from various sources. Please consult a licensed professional before attempting any techniques outlined in this book.

By reading this document, the reader agrees that under no circumstances is the author responsible for any losses, direct or indirect, which are incurred as a result of the use of information contained within this document, including, but not limited to, — errors, omissions, or inaccuracies.

"You haven't had the chance to choose the parents you have found, but you can choose which parent you want to be."

Marian Wright Edelman

TABLE OF CONTENTS

INTRODUCTION

First off, I would like to congratulate you for choosing *Bringing Up Boys: Positive Parenting Strategies to Raise Worry-Free Sons in an Anxious World*. I hope that you find the information within helpful in raising your son to be a well-adjusted, respectful young man.

When it comes to raising children, it is all a guessing game. All you can do is hope and pray that you are doing things right and that they will turn into decent adults. It's like baking a cake. You put in all of the ingredients that you are supposed to, but you won't know how it turns out until it's finished baking. Well, this book is here to help make sure you use the best ingredients possible when it comes to raising your son.

Boys and men, and almost everybody has realized, work very differently from women. Even parents say raising little girls is easier than boys. There are biological reasons for this as well as societal norms. The hardest ones to work around are societal norms. Society has made it very hard to raise boys that are comfortable with their emotions, sensitive, open, honest, and so on. Men, by society's standards, are supposed to tough and never show any emotion. If you're anything else, that must mean you're "gay".

That's really unfair to men. This book is here to show you that you can raise your sons to be open, honest, and sensitive men and that society has no right to tell you otherwise. The whole "tough man" box that men are supposed to fit into hurts their psyche. This can create issues for them in the form of emotional issues and more that they don't feel like they can talk about because it would make them look weak.

I ask you, do you want your son to feel like he can talk about anything that is bothering him, or do you want him to bottle things up until it comes out in another more dangerous way?

This book will help you do the former. We want our boys to be well-adjusted men who know how to function in society in a healthy and respectful manner. To start things off, we are going to look at the various stages of boyhood and how the male brain works differently than the female brain.

Then we will look at how to make sure you are raising your son to be respectful of women. Our kids don't learn everything from us, so we can't just expect them to view women respectfully when society tends to be hard on women.

After that, we will look at life skills and life values that you should try and instill in your sons. Then we will talk about some pretty big topics, like love, sex, affect, violence, bullying, and vulnerability.

Next, we will discuss how fathers can make sure that they are connected to their son and help ensure they become well-adjusted men. Then we will look at how mothers can do the same thing.

We will then move into looking at how to make sure your son knows how to handle negative emotions. While not everything in this chapter may be a negative emotion, they are byproducts of not handle such emotions. This will include things like anxiety, depression, and destructive behavior.

Then we will look at how media can affect the mind of your son. As much as we hate to admit it, a lot of what our children learn comes from the media, especially social media. Knowing how media affects their minds can help us to offset its effects.

After that, we'll discuss some ways to make sure your sons have a healthy heart, mind, and body. Basically, how to make sure your son is a well-rounded person. Then we will look at how important it is to encourage your son and to help him engage in healthy competition.

The next two chapters will discuss mistakes and failures. As much as parents hope to protect their children from a setback, they are inevitable. That's why it is so important to teach them how to learn from their failures and turn mistakes into successes.

Then we will talk about how to make sure your son is ready for college. Lastly, we will go over how to make sure you and your son have hope for the future, and how to make letting go a bit easier.

Being a parent is the best, most rewarding, horrible job in the world. While it won't ever be easy, we can learn some things that might just make it a little less difficult.

CHAPTER 1: THE STAGES OF BOYHOOD

There will be many, many times during your son's life, that you will ask, "What is happening with him?" This question, or a variation of it, gets asked repeatedly at certain stages of boyhood. No matter if you have a boy or girl, there are going to be some development stages that tend to be trickier to traverse than others. But, when you have some understanding of what your son is going through, you can start to appreciate that your little boy or your adolescent boy is responding to some big, often invisible, changes that are going on inside of them.

I want to make sure you understand this as well. These stages of boyhood are not necessarily the same for every single boy out there, but it applies to most. If you find that your son doesn't go through things the way we will discuss, it doesn't mean that there is anything wrong with him.

One of the scariest statistics is that you little boys' survival before year one is at a greater risk than little girls'. Boys are at a greater risk of dying prenatally, at birth, and during the first

12 months than girls. There isn't a huge difference, but it is still significant.

There has been a lot of research performed on male vulnerability in terms of health and wellbeing. As they continue to do research, it brings forward more evident that girls develop more thoroughly and faster than boys from conception.

You can ask any woman who had brothers, and they will likely tell you that they weren't as tough or brave as many people believe men should be. While they may naturally have larger muscles than girls, it doesn't mean they are inherently tougher. Physical strength may be helpful, but emotional and mental strength plays a big part in cognitive abilities, especially when comes to linguistic capacities and decision-making.

While there are early differences you have to face for most boys, the first tricky window in boyhood is toddlerhood.

Toddlerhood

Every single toddler out there, be it boy or girl, is wired to be an explorer, adventurer, and scientist using their senses in order to discover how everything in the world works. Boy toddlers have more energy and greater physical strength, which makes them extra exhausting.

It often seems as though they launch off of our laps and into the world suddenly. Every toddler wants to explore their surroundings, but boys have a greater hunger to touch whatever they can see, or tap everything they see with a toy or object. We needn't forget all of the running, jumping, and pushing they do when given just an inch of freedom.

You will likely notice that your boy has turned into a mountain climber once they reach their toddler years. You will likely find them on top of a bunch of different areas in your house that you don't want them to be. It's a good idea to make sure things are fastened to the wall, like dressers, so that they don't end up toppling over if your boy decides to scale them.

You may also find that they like to smear their food over your nice, clean walls, but this shouldn't be seen as wrong or bad. They are simply using their senses to discover meaning in their world. When they choose to use a Sharpie to draw you a pretty picture of your dog on the wall, again, they aren't doing something bad or wrong. Whatever they do during this time comes from a place of love, and they are learning how things work. That doesn't mean you can't tell them they shouldn't do that, but you shouldn't make them feel bad for having done so.

When you are faced with these moments of learning, try to follow these four steps:

1. Take a moment and make sure that you are fully present.

2. Get down on your toddler's level, and using a very positive voice, ask them, "did you do that all by yourself?" This will help to acknowledge how creative and clever they are.

3. Then you can provide them some constructive feedback. If they smeared their food along the walls, you could say something like, "We don't smear our food along the walls because we need to eat the food for energy." Or you could say, "We don't use these like this."

4. Then let your little explorer know that they will be cleaning up the mess they created. You will want to make sure that this clean up takes as long as possible because this will act as a natural inhibitor to them doing it again.

The Fierce Fours

Things don't slow down during childhood. Once they move through their toddler years, they hit right into their fours. Around four years old, boys will often appear more "badly behaved," incredibly energetic, and less responsive to their parents. This is when parents tend to get the most exasperated by their children because nothing seems to be working.

Simply put, by four, boys have more muscle, which translates to more strength. This creates a hunger to channel all of their biological drives to become warriors.

There is another possible explanation for this behavior change. It could be due to shifts in their hormonal activity, especially the luteinizing hormone. This hormone tells their testes to create Leydig cells. Their characters are hidden deep within your little boy's body to have a much larger role once they reach puberty. However, this change in hormones can play a part in why they act differently at this age.

From what I have experienced, most four-year-old boys tend to still be struggling with verbal communication and will often respond to things with physical action. This means that their movement is their language. No matter what the reason is for this increased energy and need for movement, boys between the ages of four and six will often need more freedom where they can move and lots of opportunities to be brave and adventurous. You will also want to give them some time when they have the change to autonomous and make their own choices.

This window will close, but trying to contain their natural energy and need to navigate their world with enthusiasm and very little thought is often where we damage boys and how they view themselves. Moms tend to find this particularly difficult because it becomes frustrating and exhausting to find a balance between being "loving" and "mean." Dads may become frustrated as well; however, they will often appreciate their son's need for physical freedom.

If you have a big backyard that you can fill up with a sandbox, balls, bats, and other toys, you can allow your son and his friends to run and play as much as they want. And don't be surprised if they choose to do this completely naked, and when it's cold. You will need to resist your urge to bring them inside to get them dressed and warm. They will know when they need to come in.

Let me reiterate; this very frustrating and energetic phase will pass. If you know that you are going to have to take your son somewhere public where they need to behave, give them a few hours before had to play, run, and go crazy so that they can get rid of as much energy as possible.

Given the fact that many children are now spending more time on electronic devices instead of running around outside, it is very understandable why we see more boys getting kicked out of schools at these young ages.

It is very important that you allow your sons to have plenty of physical activity and with other children their age. This need for movement will settle. It is also important to know that self-regulation will take longer to develop than it does for girls. Try to resist the urge to shout "no" to your young warriors all the time, especially if they aren't doing anything intentionally wrong. Their thinking and doing come later in life. You will often find yourself asking, "what was he thinking?" during this phase.

You may want to make sure you have plenty of coffee, tea, or chocolate put aside for yourself until this phase passes.

Sensitive Eights

Some boys will have an emotional shift around the age of eight. For some, it may seem completely out of character for them. I have met many parents who have said their eight-year-old ending up disappointing himself because he didn't do well on a spelling test or that he can't climb a tree-like he wanted to. You may find that when they experience an upset at this age, they collapse in tears fueled by self-loathing and despair. Some parents have even had their sons say that they wish they could die. This, as you would imagine, is very frightening and distressing for teachers and parents.

While it is important not to do this at any stage of boyhood, it is especially important that during this stage, you avoid telling your son to "toughen up," quit "being weak," or any other shame-based statement. Saying these things to your some teaches them that being vulnerable is something they need to avoid, fear, or hide.

Only recently has research uncovered some reasons as to why this emotional shift happens around eight. According to one long-term study performed at Melbourne's Murdoch Institute of 1200 boys, a hormonal stage known as adrenarche takes place, which causes boys to struggle emotionally. It seems as if this may be an early stage in preparation for puberty.

It is incredibly important that you are reassuring and supportive of your son during this stage. Now, if your parental instincts are telling you that something more than biology is causing your son to act differently, then, by all means, talk with your child's doctor. For the majority of boys, they will return to the boy you know in a few years before they fully hit puberty. Make sure that you enjoy that window of time.

12+ (Puberty)

This is the one window of change that every parent is anticipating, simply because it has been going on since the beginning of time. While there will be a huge surge in testosterone, about an 800% increase from toddlerhood, puberty should be viewed as a time of change and transformation, and not simply a time to dread.

Puberty causes hormonal, social, emotional, cognitive, and physical changes. This means we, as parents, have to be more mindful of the fact that all of these changes going on at one time can create a lot of stress for our boys.

When these changes start to take place during early adolescence, it can often feel like an alien has taken over your boy, and he will become insensitive to the world, grumpier, moodier, more disorganized, and forgetful. This is all completely normal and it is far out of his control to simple "be more thoughtful," or "snap out of it."

From age 12 to 15 is a very confusing journey and a time of great vulnerability, mainly due to the fact society has conditioned them not to share their fears and emotions with people. Your son is going to need a loving and warm reminder to maintain personal hygiene because it will seem that he can't smell himself. Their penis will end up becoming badly behaved and unreliable, and for some of our boys, this time can mess with their ability to speak articulately. This means that those one-word responses and mumbling that sounds like he had a paper bag over his head is often just as annoying for him as it is for you. Do your best to avoid telling him to open his mouth. A change in his brain has caused this, and he will regain his ability to speak at around age 18.

Until the age of 16, boys are more susceptible to becoming addicted to various forms of temptations, include alcohol, smoking, porn, gaming, and other illicit and legal drugs. This can be a tough time for mothers who had been really close to their pre-teen boys.

Around 16 or 17, he will start to reconnect as the later puberty stages start. Make sure you are compassionate and patient and know that small, well-timed fart close to your son can be bonding and loving gesture for your boy.

18+

The last stage is when your son becomes a legal adult. Research has found that boys are often slower than girls when it comes to making the leap into the real world. This is especially true for boys who have been raised in the electronic world. The transition period has now stretched out into their early to mid-20s.

Now, the brain, specifically the prefrontal cortex, doesn't finish maturing until in our 20s. For girls, it is normally around 22 to 24, and for boys, it happens from 25 onward.

For boys who gamed a lot instead of participating in worldly activities with people, their launching point could be a time that they aren't prepared for. Making sure that you have taught them important life skills is very helpful. It's not surprising that some boys appear lazy at this age because they feel lost and need a little encouragement to move towards more positive changes.

Shaming, shouting, and criticizing him for not being motivated will only cause him to retreat more. He is afraid of failing, and not doing anything is a way to avoid failing. The really unmotivated boys sometimes turn to alcohol or risk-taking behavior to help soothe their feelings of inadequacy and separation.

All of these stages of boyhood is basically preparing your son for adulthood and require the same thing on the part of the parent. All he needs is a loving and supportive parent to help guide and teach him.

CHAPTER 2: THE BRAINS OF BOYS AND GIRLS

No one can deny the fact that girls and boys are extremely different. These differences go farther than what we see with our eyes. Researchers have found major differences between female and male brains.

Scientists normally study only four parts of the difference between female and male brains: activity, structure, chemistry, and processing. The differences in these areas can be found in all corners of the world. Scientists have found some exceptions to this "gender rule." You might know a few boys who like talking about their feelings, are extremely sensitive, and just don't fit with how "boys" do things. Just like with any difference in gender, there isn't one way of doing things that is worse or better.

Girls and boys have different ways of learning for biological reasons: their brains were created differently. Because of these differences, girls and boys perform better if given different things that stimulate their brains. The education systems today say this isn't true and denies the results of these differences. Here is a list of differences and some of the consequences.

These differences are just some general differences in the way their brains function. You have to remember that every difference will have its disadvantages and advantages.

Brain Activity and Blood Flow

One difference that is worth looking at closer is the difference in activity in the female and male brain. A female's brain gets more blood flowing, which is called "white matter processing." Due to this higher blood flow in the cingulated gyrus, it causes females to revisit and think about emotional memories more than males.

Males were created differently. Men normally reflect briefly on a memory, analyze it slightly, and move on. During this time, they might decide to change their course and do something that is completely unrelated to their feelings instead of analyzing their feelings. Because of this, others might think that boys avoid their feelings as compared to girls, or they move on to problem-solving too fast.

Structural Differences

There are many structural elements in our brains that are different in females and males. When we say "structural," we are referring to parts of the brain and how they were built and this includes their mass and size.

Females will usually have a bigger hippocampus, which is the memory center. A female's hippocampus's neural connections are of a higher density and this causes them to be able to absorb more emotive and sensorial information than males can. When we say "sensorial," it means information that comes into and leaves from all the senses. If you were to write down all your observations in the next month about how males and females differ, you might realize that females can sense more of what is happening around her during the day and they can retain this information better than a man can.

Before a girl or boy is ever born, their brains get developed with different abilities. The left and right sides of the female and male brains aren't set up the same way. Basically, females normally have verbal centers on both sides, whereas males usually have a verbal center on just the left side. This is a huge difference. Girls like using more words when talking about a place, feeling, object, person, story, or incidence. Males don't have as many verbal centers and they don't have as much connectivity between their feelings or memories and their word centers. When talking about discussing their senses, emotions, and feelings at the same time, girls will always have an advantage. They normally are more interested in talking about all these things.

Chemistry

Female and male brains can process the same neurochemicals but differently because of body-brain connections that are specific to gender. One neurochemical is called serotonin. This helps us sit still. Oxytocin is a relationship bonding chemical.

Estrogen is a female reproductive and growth chemical. Testosterone is the aggression and sex chemical.

Due to the differences in how our bodies process these chemicals, males normally don't sit still for a long time, whereas females can usually sit still for hours at a time. Males have a tendency to be more physically aggressive and impulsive. Males don't process as much oxytocin as females and this keeps them from bonding to others. The main thing to remember about the chemical differences is realizing that boys will need different strategies to relieve their stress than girls do.

Processing

The male brain will use almost seven times more gray matter when doing an activity, whereas the female brain will use about ten times more white matter. What exactly does this mean?

Gray matter in the brain has one specific location. These are action or information processing centers in certain patches in a certain area in the brain. This could translate into a type of tunnel vision when they are working on something. When they are completely engaged in a game or task, they might not show any sensitivity to their surroundings or others.

The networking matrix that connects our brain's gray matter to other centers is white matter. This one major difference is the main reason you noticed that girls could transition between tasks better than boys. This white-gray matter difference might explain why once a female reaches adulthood, they are better at multitasking, where men are better at projects that take more focus.

Let's break it down farther:

Brain Rest Makes a Difference

A female's brain at rest is more active than a male's. The male brain needs more time to recharge than a female does. If a man feels frustrated or overstimulated, their amygdale will swell more. The amygdale is the aggression and anger center of the brain that has more tissue in men than women.

Multitasking Versus Focusing

A boy's basal ganglia will engage faster. This causes men to respond quickly when their environment calls for action. A boy's brain can operate with about 15 percent less blood flow that a girl's can. They have been structured to learn even when they are multitasking.

A man's brain has more gray matter. This keeps them from being a good multitasker but better at learning by doing a focused project or task. In the male brain, there won't be as much data that moves through their parietal lobe. This makes them better at "zoning out." Men are as sensitive as females.

Motivation and the Male Hormone

Puberty in males will begin between the ages of nine and 14. Their brains don't have as much oxytocin, and this causes them to be less motivated to please their peers, teachers, and parents while they try to create and keep relationships. Their cortisol level will drop faster once the stressor has gone away.

Males have a lot more testosterone. This causes them to be more self-reliant, assertive, competitive, and aggressive. A boy's testosterone help develop their body at a ratio of 15 percent fat and 40 percent muscle. By the end of their adolescence, boys will have ten times more testosterone than before puberty.

Sight and Memory

Boys tend to have better depth perception and narrow vision. The differences in female and male occipital lobes make males able to see better in brighter light. Men have smaller hippocampi, and therefore, they don't have as much memory storage to be able to recall information. Men have fewer neurons that help with intellectual memory and functions. This helps them interpret their sensory impulses in the cerebral cortexes. This causes them to process things slower.

Boys Don't Talk as Much

Boys normally speak later than girls do. Their frontal lobe will mature later and won't have as much blood flow. This could cause them to have to take more risks and have fewer communication skills. A boy's arcuate fasciculus will develop slower than females. The arcuate fasciculus is a bundle of nerve fibers that curve in their nervous systems. This helps with linguistics.

The motor area that helps to process grammar, word production, and speech called Broca's area isn't as active in males. A boy's corpus callosum is normally less dense. This doesn't allow for as much of a connection between each hemisphere. This can hinder cross talk that allows links between metaphysical and emotional thinking and rational and logical thinking.

Flight or Fight

A boy's brain is usually at rest in their brain stem. This is what directs the flight or fight response. It is more in the limbic system in females, and this helps to promote communication. This could make boys act quicker if threatened.

The amygdale in boys is larger, and this makes them more aggressive. Boys do have a larger cerebellum that helps them with motor control, coordination, and sensory perception. They also have more spinal fluid that sends messages from the body to the brain and vice versa that moves faster without as much impulse control.

The limbic system that houses the hippocampus and amygdale doesn't have as many connections in boys for their verbal processing. This doesn't allow them to have access to emotionally descriptive language. They don't respond as fast girls when responding verbally to very emotional situations or stress.

Executive Functions

The main reason why boys are quicker to touch a hot stove is that their prefrontal cortex, which helps them make decisions, is still undeveloped by the age of 12.

Wired Differently

Boys like structural and mechanical thinking more than girls.

What Science Says

What does all this mean? We might know already and may have known for many centuries. Girls and boys are different. If you were to tell a complete stranger the points below, they probably aren't going to be surprised at all. Schools still won't change their educational plans to help with the following:

- Girls aren't as strong as boys
- Girls aren't as mechanical as boys
- Girls aren't as assertive and competitive as boys
- Boys aren't as good at multitasking as girls
- Girls aren't as impulsive as boys

- Girls are better verbally than boys
- Girls don't roughhouse, aren't as aggressive, or as physical as boys

These differences that are listed above are only a sample of the way females and males think differently. Scientists have actually found about 100 differences in their brains. How important these differences are can't be overstated. Understanding these differences from a neurological standpoint will open the door to understanding the differences between girls and boys better. This also makes us question the way we support, educate, and parent our children from a very young age.

How to Help Boys be Better in Society and School?

For some of you, you might remember Dr. Spock and reading his books on how to raise your children. In this day and age, we could help boys live and do better if we only pay attention to all the science and apply it in their school and daily lives. Here are some suggestions:

- Let boys be boys
- Look for a school that would be the right fit for your child
- Get informed and respond to any differences in a positive manner

To quote Micheal Gurian: "The boys today need us in ways they haven't needed us before. They are being brought up in a complex world, and most of their developmental frameworks and support systems have crumbled. Once we bring our passionate attention to boys today, and come together to educate, support, and nurture them, we give a gift not only to them but to our culture, communities, and families. This is a time for a coordinated grassroots effort to help our sons."

CHAPTER 3: TEACHING HIM RESPECT FOR WOMEN

Historically, adults have thought it was cute when a boy would "pick" on little girls because they thought it meant that they liked her. They viewed it as some dating ritual. Times have changed, and most adults have started to see things from the view of the little girl. Even though they are children, the boy picking on the girl is simply harassing her, especially if she asks him to stop repeatedly.

In the "Me Too" world, it's time that boys are raised to respect women and learn how to take "no" or "stop" for an answer. Childhood picking may or may not be where violence begins, but it is most definitely disrespectful. Pervasive disrespect will eventually lead to harm and violence.

Childhood is where the seeds of toxic masculinity are planted, and they will continue to grow into a tangled web of misogynistic behaviors and thoughts as boy's age. While a lot of things play important roles in a boy's development of toxic masculinity, experts have said that promoting emotional health and teaching them that feminine traits are important, is a great way to prevent extremism.

Misogyny Has Become Mainstream

Our culture has shown us that it is okay to hate women. Leaders are boasting about sexually assaulting women, college students are getting a simple slap on the wrist for rape, and boys getting by with things through the statement "boys will be boys." There seems to be a universal message for boys to learn, and that it's okay for them to take out their frustrations and anger on women.

Somewhere throughout history, it becomes the fact that women are supposed to give all of their energy and attention to a man when he wants, and if she doesn't, he has every right to take it. We need to be talking to our boys about things like gender bias, sexism, and feminism, but research shows this isn't happening.

Honest and Open Conversations

The best way to overcome these attitudes and thoughts is by having honest and open conversations with your son. It is very important that you talk to boys about why they think some men act like this, and how they feel about it. It's also important to see your sons outside of the male stereotype. It's also important that you make sure he knows it is okay to be vulnerable, ask for help, and to cry.

On a very basic level, parents, and other important adults in a boy's life, need to be talking to them about respecting women and misogyny. It shouldn't simply be the platitude of "be respectful." You need to let him know what it means to be respectful and to respect women.

Teach Them Not to Categorize

Part of this conversation, you need to have with him is to teach him not to split women between good and bad. This is something that a lot of males will do. It is very important that you show and teach him how to create healthy friendships with girls from a young age. This will help him create a healthy attitude towards women.

From a very young age, parents can do a lot to help their sons feel comfortable with intimacy and knowing how to articulate the way they feel. Parents have the ability to encourage close friendships and help them develop the skills they need to be intimate and not get locked into the narrow view of masculinity.

To Degrade or Confront

It is important that you teach your son that there isn't any honor, bravery, or courage in degrading women or girls. However, there is courage and honor in creating a reciprocal and caring relationship with another person, as well as standing to people when they are misogynistic or degrade a woman.

This all goes back to making sure your some is emotionally literate. You want to make sure that you teach your son how to talk about his feelings. He needs to understand all types of emotions, not just angry, sad, or happy. There is a lot of complex and complicated emotional terrain that children need to learn how to understand.

Monitor Media

Violence is a lot more common in the media and has a large impact on people who view it. While boys around age five don't particularly enjoy violence, once they reach nine or ten, they are more interested in it. Having bonding time with your child by watching pay-per-view wrestling, boxing, or MMA fights only exacerbates violent attitudes.

Letting young children watch things like *Game of Thrones* or other shows with gratuitous violence and sex doesn't help things either. Video games like *Counter-Strike*, *Call of Duty*, and *Grand Theft Auto* also glorify violence against women. There are some studies that have found people who view these violent forms of entertainment on a regular basis show less kindness or empathy. Minimizing their exposure to such things between the ages of 5 and 12 will help. Over the age of 12, you can help teach them that those things aren't the norm and talk about the issues of them.

Pre-Arm Porn Exposure

The average age when a boy is exposed to pornography is age 11. This isn't *Playboy* circa 1980. Instead, it's hardcore and violent and teaches boys that women are simply here to be sexually disrespected. At around eight or nine, you need to start pre-arming your boy.

Let them know that porn exists, that there are people who may want to show it to them, that some may view it as funny, and this it can teach you bad things. Teach them that what porn depicts isn't real and is in no way a reflection of a functional and healthy relationship. They also need to understand they should talk to you if anybody tries to show it to them.

You should never normalize porn exposure as something "every boy does." This type of attitude plays a big part in the disrespect and domestic violence problem.

Call Them On It

First, let me make it clear that there are a right way and wrong in doing this. You want to show respect, so you should not shame them. Instead, let them know what they said or did was disrespectful to women.

It was very common, especially when I was young, for people say that a "woman's place is in the kitchen," along with other derogatory statements. This was normal for men to do. Guess what, things have changed.

If you catch your son criticizing women because of the way they drive or her inability to do math, call them out on it. Let them know that it is cool or funny to be sexist.

No matter what you say to your son, the biggest impact will be how they see you act. If the men they have in their lives show them, it's okay to whistle and stare at women, abuse them, objectify them, and call them names, the odds are stacked against your son with these poor examples.

You have to make sure that he is surrounded by good examples and that he feels comfortable talking about things.

CHAPTER 4: IMPORTANT LIFE SKILLS

You might be wondering how independent your child is. If you were to leave your child alone for some time, will they be able to look after themselves? Is your child equipped with the right skill to face the world?

There is a lot more for a child to learn than just academics. It doesn't matter how many activities you make them do either. No need to worry, below you will find a list of important life skills that any child needs to know. If your child can't function properly, they won't have the life skills or personality traits that develop along with them.

Educating your child on life skills can't stop with what their school exposes them to. In order to see how important these are, they have to be taught at home through activities and experience.

If your child is going to grow up strong, you have to teach them by example. It is hard being a parent. It is even harder to work on your own self-improvement, all while you are raising your own child.

Let's look at some skills that are necessary for any child to know to help them deal with adulthood. Let's find out how you can help your child learn these skills:

Adaptability and Resilience

One important skill any child needs to know is resilience. You can do this by making sure you don't give your child all the solutions.

Give your child power by letting them find the solution to their problems by themselves so that they can face any challenge that might come up. They have to learn resilience to help them adapt to different environments and changes.

Be sure you create an open communication channel to know what is happening to your child and help them when they need it. You need to model resilience, so your child knows what it looks like.

Look at a Situation from Another's Perspective

If your child comes to you with a problem that they encountered with a friend or even a problem they saw, help them look at it from another person's perspective.

Every chance you get, explain to your child a person's emotional reaction. Tell them why someone might be angry or sad. This will help them increase their ability to solve problems. It can also help them understand the people they are around.

Traveling Basics

Other than knowing how to navigate, your child needs to know the basics of traveling. They need to learn how to ride a bicycle and use public transportation. Be sure they know all these things along with being able to navigate through their neighborhood.

Show them how to purchase a bus, train, and subway tickets. Tell them which bus, train, or subway can get them from their home to their school. This is an important skill your child will need later on in life or if an emergency arises.

Washing Their Clothes

Let them help you with the household chores like laundry. Show them how to separate out the clothes, the right amount of detergent, which setting to put the washing machine on, and how to turn it on. They also need to know how to use the dryer. Make sure you show them how to clean out the lint filter. Dryers can't dry clothes if they can't breathe.

Using Maps

If you decide to take a trip, show your child the route, you would have taken. Get a map of your neighborhood and show them the best way to get from your house to their school.

Make sure your child knows how to read a map. You can also teach them how to use GPS, but map reading is becoming a lost art.

Ordering at Restaurants and Etiquette

Your child needs to know the right way to behave when in a restaurant. They also need to know how to order. You can let them decide what they would like to eat and then give the server their order.

Show them how to eat using a fork and knife. Show them how to put the fork and knife on their plate when they are finished eating. Teach them how to figure a tip to give to your server.

Household Chores and Basic Cleaning

Every parent is probably thinking the same thing right now: "How in the world can I get my child involved in cleaning?" It is hard to get your child to clean. Everyone will agree with me on this one.

Begin by asking them to please put their toys away when they have finished playing with them. Show them how to make their bed and ask them to make it up every morning. Help them find a place for all their things and ask them to keep everything put away where it goes.

You can also ask them to help you clean the dishes after eating, too. They might not be able to use a large vacuum cleaner, but on your cleaning days, give them a dust cloth and ask them to dust tables or shelves that are within their reach. When it is time to take out the trash, ask them to do it. Show them how to put it inside the large garbage bins and place the lid on securely.

When it is time to set the table, ask them to help you. You could even let them set the table in any fashion that they would like. Allow them to get creative.

Interacting with Others

We have taught our children from a very early age about "stranger danger," but this doesn't make a whole lot of sense because if we think about the people we are close to now, they were strangers to us at one point in life.

Rather than teaching them that everybody is a stranger, teach them to do what adults do. Show them how to see the difference between bad and good people. Show them ways to interact with good people.

Show them ways to make friends. Show them how to be friendly and how they need to interact with others. If you stop and think about it, any task that is done during the day is normally an interaction between two or more people. If we don't teach this to our children when they are young, they might not develop good social skills.

Independently Finish Their Tasks

Allow your child to do their own work. Allow them to choose their own backpack, make their bed, and if they are old enough, they can make their own lunch.

You can help them with this by making every task exciting. Let them pick out some new bedding and pillows with their favorite sports team, superhero, cartoon character, or whatever they love on them.

Create "stations" in your kitchen where your child can help themselves like a pancake or sandwich station. They get to choose what spread, syrup, jams, fruits, etc. so they can fill their plate with things they like to eat. They will eat more when they get to decide what's on their plate.

You could also look into some subscription activity boxes like "Little Passports" or "Flintobox" that help your children develop skills independently. The activities in these boxes are very educational. Your child will learn life skills and concepts by playing.

Preserving the Environment

We have to instill how important our environment is at a very early age. We have to teach them how to sustain our planet. Explain to them why we need to preserve our environment. Just making even the smallest changes to our lifestyle can make a big difference. Show them how to practice some earth-friendly habits in whatever they decide to do.

You can help them do some environmental activities like picking up trash in the park or planting a garden. If you are lucky enough to have your own yard, give them a section to plant anything they would like.

Show them how to dig up the soil, plant the seeds, and water the plants. Tell them it is their responsibility to make sure the soil is watered so the seeds will sprout. If you don't have a yard, you could buy them some pots and some potting soil.

Let Them Cook

Any child can cook if you let them.

You can begin with something simple. Show them how to make their own favorite sandwich, whether it is bologna and cheese or peanut butter and jelly. Show them how to butter bread to make toast.

Get some salad fixing together and let them help you put a salad together. They can tear up the lettuce, squeeze a lemon for dressing, add the chopped up vegetables to the bowl. Show them how to toss the ingredients together and let them give everyone a serving.

They can even help you with your baking. They can hand you each ingredient that you need while you do the mixing. They can help you keep the counter or table clean while you are working at the hot stove.

Shopping for Groceries

You need to always take your child with you when you go shopping for groceries. When your child knows where everything is located, you can give them their own basket and ask them to go find a few things.

You can give your child some things that they are responsible for each month, like their fruit juices or snacks. Give them money and let them pay for the items. The most important thing is that YOU have to model smart shopping for them. They learn by watching what you do.

Budgeting and Managing Money

This is very basic. Give your child a weekly allowance that they need to use for things that they need.

If they want to buy something that costs more money than what they have, tell them they are going to have to save their money until they have enough to buy the item.

You can "cut them a deal" by letting them borrow the money from you. You could ask them to save their money for a certain number of weeks and then match the amount of money they have saved with the same amount. This will motivate them to save money.

You also need to teach them how to comparative shop. Show them how to look at the products you need and find a cheaper alternative if it is possible. If they would like to buy some things the next time you go shopping, encourage them to find the cheaper alternative of a product you need.

This type of budget training creates a habit within your child not to waste money. Any child that is over ten years old needs to understand how important money managing is.

Children get introduced to the money concept around seven years old through math at school, but no one teaches them how important and relevant saving, planning, budgeting, and how valuable money really is. They can't know these things unless they actually handle the money in real life.

You could open a bank account in your child's name and have them add a specific amount of money to it each month. This could be money they get for birthdays, from doing chores, or helping out their neighbors. This will help show them how to appreciate money even more.

Making Decisions

Choosing a life partner, career, or education, there are countless decisions that we are going to need to make during our lives. We need to teach our children this skill early on in their lives. It is very easy to do: you can teach them in simple but small ways on ways to make smart decisions. Begin by having them choose between two games or activities, two types of clothes, or two different foods.

When this happens, your child will begin to understand the consequences that all their decisions made. Help them through this process. Show them how to weight the disadvantages and advantages before they make a decision.

Time Management

You might be wondering how to do this yourself. You can teach your child how to do this by helping them claim responsibility for their time.

This can be done by buying them an alarm clock for them to use to help them get up on time so they won't be late for school, so you don't' have to wake them up all the time.

Buy them a planner so they can keep track of their school work or other activities so they can keep track of their time and what they need to do and what time it has to be done by.

By doing this, they will start to set aside certain times of the day for chores and playing.

Let Them Do It By Themselves

Every parent has to face it: our children are going to grow up and leave home to get an education and pursue their career of choice. If they haven't been taught to take responsibility and the right skills, it might cause some huge problems for them later in their life.

Many parents run all over town, doing whatever their children need them to do. They don't let their children get involved in anything. They might even go so far as to have their science projects professionally made. This shouldn't ever be the case.

Whether it is taking their plate to the kitchen, packing their backpack, just make sure your child is responsible for their own work. They have to be taught these skills now. You can't wait until they are headed off for college to tell them how to do things. Do it now, and you will have another set of hands to help you.

Health and First Aid

You might not always be around when your child gets a rash, bit, or hurt. You need to empower them so that they can take care of themselves in case there is an emergency until they have reached adulthood.

This is something that schools should cover but doesn't. Since schools won't do it, you have to. You need to teach your child simple first aid. This is easily done by getting a first aid kit and going through its contents with your child. Tell them what everything is and what it is used for. Children are great at learning things. We just don't give them enough credit.

Another good skill is teaching your child how to take care of their health. Rather than forcing them to eat their vegetables, tell them how risky it is to their health to only eat junk food. Tell them that junk food could hurt their health. Explain how healthy foods can benefit them in many different ways.

If your child is interested in sports, tell them about what foods will give them more agility and stamina that will help them play their sport better.

If your child is interested in their appearance, tell them about foods that contain Omega 3 fatty acids that will help with hair, skin, and nails.

Self Defense

I am sure that you will agree that in the world today, safety is very important. Helping your child learn some self-defense will make your child feel more confident and independent.

This is a must, whether it is for girls or boys. Many schools will teach a course in basic self-defense for children. If your child's school doesn't, try to find a class at your local community center. You might even find one that offers family classes.

In conclusion, when your child reaches about seven years of age, they have already developed a foundation for their personality. The above life skills can enhance their positive personality traits.

Your child, by this point, should be independent in the way they function inside the house. They need to be following all the rules that you have given them, which will help build the traits of reasoning and understanding.

Every parent needs to teach their child how to work hard, believe in themselves, persistence, patience, positivity, and kindness. Developing life skills is necessary so your child will have an idea of what they would like to do with their lives and to help them be the person they would like to be.

Let's educate our children in ways that are entertaining and fun so that we don't have to worry about their skills or morals.

CHAPTER 5: IMPORTANT LIFE VALUES

Besides making sure your son understands basic life skills, there are also life values that they need to have. These values help them to be decent adults who take responsibility for their actions. While most of these values will need to be taught throughout their childhood, there are some who can make sure they understand from a young age. While a lot of parents think that it's premature to teach values to preschoolers or toddlers, I believe there is no such thing. The first five values we will go through can and should be taught by age five.

Honesty

Start teaching your child at a very young age what it means to be honest and tell the truth. The best way to do this is to be truthful yourself. Think about this. Paula decided that she needed to limit the play dates between her three-year-old and his friend. They had been getting into fights recently, and Paula thought they needed some time apart. When Greg's mother called on an evening to arrange a play date, Paula said that Charles was sick.

Charles overheard this and asked, "Am I sick? What's wrong?" Paula, surprised by her son's concern, told him that she had only said he had been sick because she didn't want to upset Greg's mother. Paula then started to explain the difference between different types of lies, which confused Charles. All he got from it was that fibbing could be okay and that it was something people often did.

Children take cues from their parents, so you need to avoid deception, even if it seems innocent. For example, telling your son, "Let's not tell Daddy about…" Allow your child to see you being honest with others. It would have been better if Paula has simply been honest and told Greg's mom why she thought they need to a break.

Another good way to instill honesty is to make sure you don't overreact if your child does lie. Instead, you need to help them figure out how to tell you the truth. When you do this, you let your child know that, while being honest may not always be comfortable, everybody always feels better when you tell the truth. It's also important that you don't overreact when they tell the truth. One of the main reasons kids will lie is because they were yelled at or scolded for telling the truth.

Justice

It's important that you teach your child how to make amends. Let's look at this example. James and Michelle, four-year-old cousins, were building castles from blocks. Suddenly, James

57

knocked over the castle Michelle had built, and she started to cry. James' father saw what happened and told his son to apologize. James quickly said, "I'm sorry."

Then his dad took him aside and asked why he destroyed the castle. He said that he was mad at Michelle because her castle was bigger. His dad said that wasn't an excuse for destroying his cousin's castle, but said he understood his feelings. He then sent him back to play.

This father's reaction was typically a reaction to any psychologically savvy parent. He helped his son identify and express how he felt and understand why he felt that way. This is a good this, but there is more that he could have done. In order to help your son to internalize justice, parents should also encourage their child to help fix the wrong. For example, James' dad could have suggested that James help Michelle rebuild the castle.

It's fairly easy to get a child to say "I'm sorry" because it lets them off the work without making them think about what they did. Teaching your child how to make amends for wrongs they have done will teach them a stronger message.

Determination

Encourage your child to take on challenges. Determination can easily be encouraged, starting at a very young age. One of the easiest ways to do so is to avoid excessive praise and to give them honest feedback that is delivered in a supportive way.

Another way to encourage determination is to encourage your child to do things that may not come all that naturally to them, and then praise them for trying. If your son tends to be shy, encourage them to talk to other kids on the playground, even if he feels scared. If he tends to get angry quickly, teach him ways to diffuse his anger. Always congratulate your child when they are able to do something that was difficult.

Consideration

Teach your son how to be considerate of other people's feelings. Carol was completely frustrated because of her sons, aged three and four, would end up fighting and whining every time they went grocery shopping. She decided to sit them down and say that they all need to figure out what they could do when they went shopping so that nobody would end up feeling upset.

Carol asked for suggestions on how to make grocery shopping a better experience. Her four-year-old said that they should bring snacks so that they wouldn't start begging for cookies. Her three-year-old said that he could sing quietly so that he would feel happy.

The boys kept their promises, and their next grocery trip went a lot better. The youngest boy, as they left the store, asked his mom, "Do you feel really upset?" Carol assured him that she was fine and remarked how nice it had been that nobody had gotten into an argument.

Doing these little problem-solving exercises does help your child learn consideration. With time, even the youngest child will notice actions or words can help make a person smile or feel good, and that when they are nice to somebody, that person will be nice back.

Love

A lot of parents have this belief that children are naturally generous and loving with their affection. While this is partially true, for this love to last, it also needs to be reciprocated. It's sad to know that during the course of a day, the phrase "I love you" is the one a child is least likely to hear.

Your child needs to see you demonstrate love and affection for others. Hug and kiss your partner, especially when your child can see. Talk with your children about how much you appreciate and love their cousins, uncles, aunts, and grandparents, as well as them.

Show your child love in cute ways. Put a note in his lunchbox. Tape up a heart on their bathroom mirror. Give them hugs. Don't let those frantic mornings and evenings push loving gestures for your day.

The more you say "I love you" to your son, the more they are going to say it back. The more kisses and hugs you give, the more you will notice your home is filled with affection and love. When our children feel like they can freely express love to us, we have instilled in them the greatest value.

Time Management

Being a success is strongly connected to having great time-management skills. We need to teach our children that they should take care of their most important task first. It is very natural to want to avoid things that cause stress, but if you take the time to teach your child to get the most stressful thing done first, the rest of the work they have to do will go by much easier.

When children get caught up in little, unimportant tasks, it will pull them away from tasks that are more important. Within this, it is also important to make sure your child knows how important it is to be on time, or early, to commitments. Nobody likes people who are always late. Teach them that being on time helps others to respect them and view them as dependable.

Self-Care

Complacency and personal power cannot live together. Parents need to teach children how to dedicate their time and energy when they need to, to make sure that no important areas of what they need to do are being neglected.

They deserve having time for work and free-time, where they can take some time to feel free from the weight of the things they have to do. The best way for you to teach your child how to keep them balanced is to require them to place their responsibilities first and free-time second. This value will help them to manage their lives in an efficient way. Have free-time second prevents your child's free-time from being bogged down by responsibilities that haven't been finished.

CHAPTER 6: TEACHING HIM ABOUT LOVE, SEX, AND AFFECTION

How many times each day do you hug your child?

Everybody lives a stressful, busy life. We all have countless concerns about our children, but one thing is clear: we all need to take some time and give our children a big squeeze. Research has found a link between childhood affection and their happiness and health in the future.

Science says that affection and warmth that are given to children can result in positive outcomes for them. Fewer behavioral and psychological problems, better communication, improved academic performance, and higher self-esteem have been linked to this kind of affection. But children who don't have parents that show them affection normally have low self-esteem and feel anti-social, aggressive, hostile, and alienated.

Many studies have been done that show the relationship between a child's success and happiness and parental affection.

Researchers from Duke University did a study in 2010 with attentive mothers and their babies. These babies grew up to be less anxious, more resilient, and happier adults. The study watched 500 people from the time they were infants until they reached their 30s. Psychologists watched how the mothers interacted with their babies during several tests for development.

The researchers rated that attention and affection level on a five point rating scale from being "negative" to being "extravagant." About six percent showed very high levels of affection, 85 percent showed a normal amount of affection, and ten percent of all the mothers show a low level of affection.

Once 30 years were up, those same people were then interviewed on their emotional health. The people whose mothers showed either a caressing or extravagant affection weren't as likely to feel anxious or stressed. They also reported less psychosomatic symptoms, distressing social interactions, and hostility.

The psychologists that were involved in this study found that oxytocin might be responsible for this outcome. Oxytocin is a chemical found in the brain that gets released when people feel a connection and love. It can help a parent bond with their child. This just adds more support and trust between them. A bond like this can help our brains release and use oxytocin, and this causes a child to feel better, positive emotions.

Another study done at UCLA in 2013 found that affection and unconditional love from parents could make children less anxious and happier. This occurs because the brain can change due to this affection. If there is a lack of affection and childhood abuse, it can impact the child both physically and mentally. This could lead to all sorts of emotional and health problems during their lives. What is even more fascinating is scientists think that parental affection could protect children against childhood stress and all its harmful effects.

Another study done at the University of Notre Dame in 2015 found that children who received affection were a lot happier during adulthood. Over 600 adults took a survey about the way they were raised. The survey included the amount of physical affection they received. The ones who reported receiving lots of affection during childhood has less anxiety and depression and were more compassionate. The people who had less affection had mental health problems, get upset quicker in a social situation, and couldn't relate to another person's perspective.

Studies have also been done about the effects of skin on skin contact for babies. This interaction between baby and mommy can help calm the baby, so they don't cry as much and it helps them sleep more. It can also boost brain development. Children who grew up in an orphanage had high levels of cortisol as compared to children who grew up in a loving home.

Researchers believe the lack of physical contact is the main factor in these physical changes.

There have been many studies done about the effects of massage. All of them show that massage has many positive benefits for children, especially reducing anxiety. Massage is a wonderful way for a parent to connect with their child on both an emotional and physical level. Beginning during infancy if a parent starts massaging their child regularly, it can create a strong, lasting bond. Studies show that adults and children who received massages experienced less anxiety during hospital stays, academic stress, and any other stressful time.

So, have you hugged your child today?

From the time you bring your child home, make sure you rock, touch, and hold them. Spend countless moments caressing their skin with your hands. As they begin to age, make sure you are playful and do fun activities like making up silly games or dancing together.

Set yourself a reminder to make hugging a normal part of your routine. If you watched the movie *Trolls*, they wore watches that would alarm every hour so they could get a hug. If this is what it is going to take for you to get or give a hug, then go ahead and set an alarm. Be sure to give your children a hug throughout the day, like before leaving for school, when they come home from school, and right before they go to bed.

You could also use affection when you need to discipline your child. While talking with them about what they did that was wrong, place your hand on their shoulder, and then hug them when you are through talking to them to make sure that they know even when they do something wrong, you never stop loving them. If your child hits another child, give them a hug and explain how hugging is better than hitting.

Just be careful and don't start smothering your child. Respect their comfort level and make sure you change as they get older.

How to Teach Your Child About Affection and Love

Learning ways to express healthy affection and love is necessary for a child to have a good sense of self-respect and self-esteem.

Here are some tips on ways to teach your child how to receive and express affection and love:

- Teach your child about different kinds of relationships, including romantic or intimate relationships, affectionate and loving relationships, and courtesy or respectful relationships and ways to show healthy affection and love in every one of them. This is all depending on age and is important for safety and setting healthy boundaries.

    o   Romantic or Intimate Relationships

These types of relationships might happen during adolescence once a child starts learning how to love and affection are received by others. There are normally natural emotions that happen. If your child asks you questions or shares their experiences, they are looking for validation and trying to understand the way they are feeling and ways to express affection and love in a healthy, loving, respectful, and intimate manner.

○   Affectionate or Loving Relationships

These types of relationships are associated with people who are close to a child like a caregiver or family member and people who are always around the child most of the time. Expressing affection and love to these people might be more enhanced by hugging, kissing, and embracing or being held. This is shown by parents toward one another, but by parents by telling their child they love them, listening to their child, and playing with the child or any combination of these. Just remember to be mindful of your language and tone of voice.

○   Courteous or Respectful Relationships

These types of relationships will have an authority figure involved who asks their child to have etiquette and teaching them to say, "I'm sorry," "thank you," and "please." There might also be times when a child helps another child who has fallen and needs help by going to them and asking if they can help in any way.

- Teach your child to love their bodies by getting enough exercise, eating healthy, and having healthy hygiene. This helps them develop a platform early on in their lives for self-respect and self-esteem. This is what fuels their desire to express healthy affection and love toward others.

- Teach your child how to use appropriate language and discipline them anytime they use inappropriate language. Children have a knack of picking up language from home, television, school peers, and social media. Teach them ways to express themselves by helping them describe their opinions and feelings without using vulgar language in place of appropriate adjectives.

- Teach your child to be aware of other people's diversity and customs and ways that this could affect how they express affection and love. We are living in times that are constantly changing, and some of these changes are transgender, gender equality, and gender in general. It might be about restrooms or same sex parents but they need to learn the value of their own philosophies about these diverse considerations.

- Teaching your child rules and keeping those rules along with healthy boundaries are ways to show healthy affection and love, and they will be using them in their lives for many years to come. Children will be able to set healthy boundaries with others and then express their feelings when these boundaries get crossed.

- Teach your child to find comfort from you of someone else who is supportive and trustworthy. Children need somebody they can go to that that can trust and respect. It might not always be the parent who is available during these times. Therefore, your child needs someone who is willing to talk to them and work with them when they need comforting. Their list of people needs to be one that is approved by you, the parent, and who they feel safe with.

- Teach your child ways to listen before they speak. Listening is another skill that takes focus and attention. This is best taught by validating their feelings and having them learn to validate your feeling or someone else's feelings. This is learned by paying attention, repeating the things you say, and understanding another person's perspective. This is, of course, age appropriate but very important for their future relationships. Here is an example conversation:

  - Mom: "How do you think Dave felt when you took his pen without asking first?"
  - Child: "Mad."

o   Mom: "Do you think you can tell Dave that you understand that he felt mad when you too his pen?"

A child might speak to you straightforward and directly. They might not be as aware as an adult is about how to act in these situations. They have to learn how to be affectionate and love nonjudgmentally. This is the key to creating healthy affection and love toward others.

Parents are a necessary part of teaching by modeling their behavior with others. Traits like being compassionate, loyal, honest, being considerate, and having integrity are some things your child is going to observe and then model it within their own lives.

What You Need to Teach Your Son About Sex

Talking to your child about sex is the hardest part of them growing up. This is because none of us have had a good conversation about it with our parents and so we don't have the faintest clue about how to do it. Since most of our knowledge about sex comes from experiences, stories from friends, and what we've seen on television, this means there is a lot of things we know, but we don't have a large framework when just thinking about sex. Everyone has a little bit of knowledge about this and that when talking about sex, but for some reason, these pieces just don't connect to each other.

These results aren't surprising. In every survey that has been given to either college students or high school seniors, they say that their parents never talked to them about sex. What's worse is that many of the ones who had the talk, their conversation only lasted about ten minutes. Things are a lot harder for boys than girls because they are less likely to have a conversation with their parents. If they do, it is very short and will only cover a few topics. Here is a short list of things your child will need to know. I am writing as if I am talking to my son but all I say will apply equally in a conversation with a girl.

The average American teenager will lose their virginity about 16, and only a handful will still be a virgin when they graduate. The normal age for marriage is mid to late 20s for most American females so this means that your child will have sex for around one decade before they are married. This means your child will have more than one partner before they are married.

1.   Values

Your job is helping your son develop their sexual ethics; this will guide their behavior. The best way to do this is by connecting it to values you have already taught them such as care, honesty, and respect. These things might look a bit different when practices with strangers, friends, extended family, and immediate family; they are probably going to look a bit different here.

2. Broadly focus on sexuality

You should talk about sexuality rather than sex since this is a broad term that will include various sexual behaviors and relationships. Sex only talks about a certain act and the broader things that are related to sex, and this could get very confusing.

3. Sexuality and dating are connected

Dating will inherently include some type of sexual contact like holding hands and kissing. Doing things like this in public is a way we let others know that we are dating a particular person. Holding hands, kissing, and other sexual behaviors could include messages about exclusiveness and trust. You have to talk to your son about what messages kissing sends.

4. Appropriate age to have sex for the first time

This is related to your values. You need to set an age that you think your son is going to be both emotionally and physically mature enough to engage in sex. You have to be clear with him about the age you gave him based on his values, maturity level, and who he is, combined with your perspective and experience. You have to be realistic. He is going to use anything you say to gauge his behavior and this includes deciding if he is actually ready at the age you gave him. As stated earlier, 16 is the average age.

5. Consent

Your son has to have the ability to tell his partner that he is giving them consent, and he has to hear consent from whomever he is with. He has to understand that consent is specific and the need to use words like "sex" and not expressions such as "let's do it." If your son can't explicitly tell who he's with that, he wants to have sex. He isn't ready to be having sex with anyone.

6. Refusal

Your son has to understand that it is okay for him to say "slow down," "not yet," or "no." This goes along with consent and one that is contrary to what society's expectations are for boys. Boys are always supposed to be ready for sex and will always be the ones who initiate sexual contact. Basically, he should know that he has options if his partner moves faster than he wants to go. He also needs to know that, above all, he HAS to respect his partner if they say "slow down," "not yet," or "no." NO MEANS NO and it doesn't matter who you are.

7. Basics of contraceptives

Your son should know the odds of getting pregnant and how they could be changed by using various contraceptive devices and strategies. The level of detail and specifics are totally up to you. Many people only talk about the rhythm method or tracking ovulation. You have to help your son know that contraception helps him control when he becomes a father.

Just remember that there isn't any form of contraception that is 100 percent foolproof.

8. Basics of reproduction

Your son needs to know that any time an erect penis enters a female's vagina, there is a chance of pregnancy happening. Your son has to know this even if he is gay. There is a surprising number of gay guys who have sex with a female before they realize they are gay or for many other reasons.

You and your son might be feeling a bit overwhelmed right now, and that is fine. It is way too much for just one talk. His upbringing needs to involve many talks over the course of a few years. He didn't learn to say "thank you" and "please" with just one talk.

We all dream of sending our children into the world with the knowledge of how to manage their time, how to manage money, and knowing who they are. This is why we talk about these things over and over again with them. Sexuality is just as complex as these are but we don't do as good of a job talking about them. As your son gets older, he will develop, his mental capacity increases, he gets more mature emotionally, and he is going to gain some sexual experience. Your conversations about sex need to have some experience, too. I hope the above helps you bridge that gap.

CHAPTER 7: TEACHING HIM ABOUT VIOLENCE AND BULLYING

Violence and bullying are very real things that children have to face. Children need to be taught how to face these things and handle the negative emotions associated with them.

Violence

Violence in school has become much more prevalent and is something that can frighten your child. They may not feel safe, or they could worry that their friends or loved-ones could get hurt. This fear can translate to other areas of their life, and not just at school. They will turn to you, the adult, for guidance and information on how they should react. Parents, as well as school personnel, are able to help children feel safe by creating a sense of security and normalcy and talking to them about any fears they may have.

First off, it's important to reassure your child that he is safe. Validate how they are feeling, but emphasize that they are safe. The important thing is to make sure that they feel safe to talk about everything they feel when it comes to violence, and then help them to put it into perspective.

Let any questions that they ask be your guide as to how much you tell them. Be patient with them. Children, preteens, and teens don't always freely express their feelings. Watch them for clues that they may be interested in talking, like hovering around you as you are doing things around the house. Some children like to do art projects, play music, or write as a way to let things out. Young children will need concrete activities for them to express and identify their feelings.

Any explanation of violence you provide needs to be developmentally appropriate. During early elementary school, you should keep the information simple and brief. It should be balanced with reassurances them their home and school are safe places, and that there are adults there willing to protect them. Remind them of things that schools do to help keep them safe, and also go over some things you can do in the home to protect them.

For upper elementary and early middle school aged kids, they will be more vocal in asking their questions about if they are actually safe and what is being done to ensure they are safe. You may need to help them to separate what is real from what is fake.

Upper middle and high school aged kids tend to have stronger and varying opinions about the causes of violence. They will likely share concrete suggestions about ways to make places safer and how to prevent tragedies. You can start to emphasize the role that children play in maintaining safety and home and school, and to make sure they understand the importance of safety guidelines. They also need to feel safe in sharing any personal safety concerns to the appropriate adults and getting support for their emotional needs.

It is also important that you, from time to time, review safety procedures. Make sure that your son has at least one adult in their community and at school that they feel comfortable going to when they feel at risk.

If a major violent event occurs, like a school shooting, limit their exposure to it. If the information is developmentally inappropriate, it can create confusion or anxiety, especially for young children. You should also be mindful of the conversations you have with other adults if your child is nearby, even if they are teens, and make sure you limit their exposure to angry, vengeful, and hateful comments that could be misunderstood.

Bullying

Bullying is a form of violence that your child may have to face during their life. Let's look at two children who have something in common. Every day, 10-year-old Brent would come home and ask his parents for more lunch money, but he always came home from school starving. It turned out that he was having to give his lunch money to a fifth-grader who had been threatening to beat him up.

Leslie, 13, believed things to be going well at school since the popular girls were nice. Then she discovered one of them had made up a mean rumor about her. That night, she cried herself to sleep, and then she started visiting the nurse each day complaining about her stomach hurting so that she didn't have to face the girls in study hall.

Both Brent and Leslie are facing bullying that is very widespread. Most every child and teen have said that they have been or no people who have been bullied at their school.

A bully can easily turn something simple, like going to recess or the bus stop into a nightmare. Bullying might not always leave physical scars, but they leave deep emotional scars. Bullying can go from hurtful words to violent threats, to property damage, and even physical damage.

If you find out that your child is being bullied, you will want to find a way to stop it. There are also skills that you can teach your child to help them cope with gossip, bullying, or teasing, and help lessen the lasting impact. Even if bullying hasn't touched your children, it's important that you talk to your child about it so that he is prepared if it happens.

When children have older siblings, they will likely be teased at some point. This is not typically harmful when it remains friendly, playful, and mutual, and they both find it funny. When the teasing becomes constant, unkind, and hurtful, it crosses over into bullying territory and should be stopped.

Bullying is intentional psychological, verbal, or physical harm. It could include extorting possessions and money, mocking, threats, name-calling, shoving, or hitting. There are some who shun others and spread rumors. Others hide behind social media to taunt and hurt people.

Bullying needs to be taken very seriously, and it should never be brushed off as something your child has to "deal with." The lasting effects can be very serious and can affect their self-worth and sense of safety. In some serve cases, bullying can lead to school shootings and suicides.

Unless your child actually tells you they are being bullied or see visible injuries or bruises, it can be hard to figure out what is going on. There are some warning signs you can be on the lookout for. You may notice that your child is behaving differently or seems more anxious, doesn't sleep well, doesn't eat, or stops doing things they usually enjoyed. When your child is moodier or more easily upset, or if they start trying to avoid certain situations, it could be due to a bully.

If you suspect that your child is being bullied, but they are reluctant to open up, try to find times to bring up the issue in a roundabout way. For example, you could see something on TV and use it as a conversation starter. You could say, "What do you think about that?" This could end up leading to, "Have you ever been in this situation?" You could also talk about experiences you or somebody else has had at their age.

It's important that you let your child know that if they are being bullied, or see somebody being bullied, that they should talk to someone, whether it's you, another adult, or a sibling.

When your child does talk to you about being bullied, listen to them calmly, and offer them support and comfort. Kids don't like sharing about bullying because they are embarrassed, or they are worried their parents will get upset.

Some kids feel like they brought it on themself and that they could have prevented it. They are also sometimes afraid it will get worse if the bully finds out that they told. Others think their parents won't believe them.

Let your child know that you are proud that they told you. Remind them they aren't alone, and that many people get bullied at some point. Ensure they understand the bully is the one behaving badly and not them. And let them know that you will help them figure out what to do.

Then, you will need to inform somebody at school. This could be the teacher, counselor, school nurse, or principal. They typically can monitor the situation and prevent any more problems.

Since bullying can involve many different things, there won't be a one-size-fit all approach. What could work in or situation may not in a different one. Different factors like the age of those involved, severity, and type of bullying will help to figure out what should be done.

Make sure that if your child mentions the bully telling them things will get worse if they tell anybody. It might be useful to talk to the bully's parents. In most cases, a counselor or teacher should be the first person you contact. If you want to speak with their parents, do so in a school setting with a mediator of some sort.

Once you have taken this first course of action, talk with your child about what to do if they have to face bullying:

- Do your best to avoid the bully and use the buddy system. Use a bathroom the bully doesn't hand around, and don't visit your locker when nobody is in the hall. Keep somebody with you so that you are never alone with your bully.

- Hold your anger. It's natural to become upset when bullied, but that's what the bully wants. It's what makes them feel powerful. Try to practice not getting visibly upset or crying. This will take a lot of practice, but it is a useful way to keep yourself off of a bully's radar. Try cool down tactics like counting to ten, deep breaths, or simply walking away. Sometimes it's a good idea to teach your child how to have a "poker face" until they are free from danger since laughing or smiling can end up provoking them.

- Be brave, walk away, and ignore them. In a firm and clear voice, tell them to stop and then walk away. Work with your child on ignoring hurtful remarks, like texting somebody or acting uninterested. When you ignore the bully, you show them you don't care. Eventually, they are going to get bored.
- Let an adult know.
- Talk to somebody that you trust.

It's also important, as the parent, to help rebuild your child's confidence. Bullies are really good at breaking down confidence. Make sure your child spends time with friends who are a positive influence. Above all, always be there for them when they need to talk.

Is Your Child a Bully?

As tough as this may be, you may find out that your son is bullying another child. If you don't put a stop to it, it can end up leading to more aggressive antisocial behavior and can end up hurting your child's success in school.

Kids can end up bullying for several reasons. Some do it because they feel insecure. Picking on another person who seems physically or emotionally weaker makes them feel more in control, popular, or important. Other times, kids will do it because they don't realize it is unacceptable to pick on somebody due to their religion, race, looks, or size.

There are times where bullying is simply a part of an ongoing pattern of aggressive or defiant behavior. These kids need to learn how to manage their strong, negative emotions. Professional counseling can help them with this and help to improve their social skills.

Some will bully because they are copying behaviors that they have witnessed at home. Kids who face unkind and aggressive interactions in their family learn to treat others the same way. Kids who have been on the receiving end of taunting learn that bullying is able to place them in control over a weaker person.

When you find out that your son has been bullying kids, let them know that this kind of behavior is unacceptable and that there will be consequences at school, home, and the community if it continues. Then you need to do your best to understand why they have been doing this.

It is important that you take this seriously. Let them know that you won't tolerate bullying. Establish rules and then stick to them. If your punishment involves taking away their privileges, make sure that it is meaningful. If they bully through social media or other electronic means, take away their computer and phone privileges for a while. If they act out at home, stop them. Teach them nonviolent ways to react, such as walking away.

Teach your child kindness and respect. Teach them it isn't right to ridicule people based on perceived differences, and try to instill some empathy. Think about getting involved in the community so that they are exposed to people who are "different."

Look into their social life to help figure out what could be influencing their actions. Talk with the principal, counselors, teachers, and parents of their friends. Are his friend's bullies? What pressures is he facing? Talk with him about those relationships. Put him in activities that are outside of school so that he can make other friends.

Encourage him to behave. Positive reinforcement is something that most parents never think about, yet it is more powerful than negative discipline. When your child is behaving, and when they handle rough situations in a constructive way, praise him for it.

Show him how to act. Think about how you talk around children and how you handle problems. If you instinctively act with aggression, chances are they have learned their actions from you. Instead, point out positive things in people and not negatives. When you face a conflict, be open about it is frustrating, and how you cope with that.

If you find that your son has a problem with dealing with emotions, and you have done the best you can, it might be a good idea to speak with their doctor. They can guide you in a direction to getting him, and you help.

Getting him to stop bullying won't happen overnight. Bad behaviors won't simply stop on their own. It will take time, but if you work with him, he can change his actions.

CHAPTER 8: TEACHING HIM ABOUT VULNERABILITY

Before I ever had children, I had heard all the stereotypes. All boys love sports, they like being all rough and tumble, and they are only "noise with dirt." As with any stereotypes, they normally hide some underlying truth. Boys are complex humans who actually experience a huge range of emotions.

In the past, pressures in society have placed boys into a toughness box where they get scolded for experiencing vulnerability, pain, or sadness. Even though I never thought I would buy into these stereotypes, I didn't ever see the folly of thinking like this until I had my own boy.

After I experienced a huge feeling of compassion, sensitivity, and sweetness from my boy, I can see that these stereotypes are very dangerous. Any type of mindset that puts limits on a child developing their emotions will keep them from reaching their full potential.

Nowadays, many parents are trying to raise boys to have better developed emotions. Unfortunately, we still see and hear the past telling us to not allow our boys to cry and to toughen them up.

So, how in the world are we going to help our boys regulate their emotions, develop empathy, and to understand themselves better?

Words are Powerful

Just like any other aspect of parenting, words hold a lot of power. The way we speak to our children turns into their internal dialogue. This holds true for the way they learn emotions, too.

New research shows that parents who tell their children how others feel can help create emotional skills in our children, such as empathy. It might seem silly to describe that a child is feeling sad after he fell off the jungle gym, but for a young child, other people's feeling isn't as obvious to them as they are to an adult.

Create Limits

We have to create limits on their behavior, but we don't ever need to set a limit on a child's emotions.

This could be a bit tricky during certain situations. Placing boundaries on a child's behaviors means we have to set expectations that we need to follow through on. We should expect our children to sit the right way when eating dinner. But when we try to control their emotions might make them feel like their emotions aren't important or valid.

Any parent knows they can't control their children's feelings. So, basically, it becomes a balance between creating limits on their behavior and doing it in a way that supports them emotionally.

For any child, this kind of parenting will give them the structure they need, plus it lets them have enough independence to create great skills to let them regulate their emotions.

Allow Them to Play

Some boys will have endless amounts of energy. Most of the school systems don't have a lot of time to let the children exercise and move to burn off that excess energy. Having too many limits on moving can affect how well they are able to concentrate during school, but it could harm their emotional development.

Studies have shown that children who are given more play time were more empathetic toward peers that children who weren't given any play time.

The main aspect of play time is that it has to be free play. Don't try to organize the children into teams or have them do specific activities. During free play, most children have to create their own activities or rules with each other. This is the best way for a child to create real emotional development. When adults don't try to control each aspect of what their children do, their child has to learn how to follow the rules that were set by their group or create their own limits.

This generation of parents knows that bringing up children needs to include a lot of emotional work. Boys and girls will create a better, supportive environment where they will learn how to cope with any powerful emotion that arises.

Courage and Vulnerability

Teaching boys how to share things about themselves that their friends might not know is hard to do. They don't want their friends to think they are "weak." During one seminar, a quiet little boy spoke up: "Everybody thinks that I don't do anything but sports, but I really like to sew."

If every tween boy could be this courageous, the world would be a better place. Because of all the gender stereotypes, boys have been taught that they have to act a certain way to be considered a "real boy." Most people place boys in a "blue box," and they tell them they have to play with action figures, their favorite has to be blue, and they have to love playing sports. It also teaches boys that they have to:

- Solve their problems using power, aggression, and violence.
- Rely on themselves (because asking for help show weakness)

- Keep emotions under wraps (sharing how we feel is gay and girlish)
- Being stylish is fine but too stylish means they are gay
- Be into girls, or they are gay
- Be stoic, strong, and tough

This list can go on, and on putting a boy into a "blue box" isn't terribly bad but it does limit them. It keeps them from being themselves. It also reinforces their beliefs in a hierarchy and this can lead to bullying and other way to oppress others. When little boys feel safe and they stop listening to all the ideas about how they are supposed to be, they will begin embracing their power and being who they really are. What exactly is the "power within?" It is a type of power that boys need to have in order to understand and be able to reject or question specific aspects of how they are being raised.

Types of Power

- Power Within

This is a feeling of self-worth. It gives them the ability to have integrity and not being reliant on external reinforcements or approval. The boy who has power within and isn't afraid to tell his friends that he likes to sew is very courageous. In order for a boy to have power within means, they have to be courageous, and having courage means they have to be vulnerable. The hard part is that if a boy doesn't like who they are, they won't or can't stand up for others or themselves. They also won't or can't ask for help. This type of vulnerability is what allows a boy to move away from their "blue box" and live to be who they want to be and truly are.

- Power With

This shows strength in numbers. This is earned by having a sense of community and trust. This creates alliances to find a common goal. Standing up and welcoming others who don't fit into the normal "blue box."

- Power Over

This takes from and imposes authority over other people. The "blue box" rules show how much power society has over our boys. Bullying is the best example of having power over someone else.

How can we teach these concepts to our boys?

- Tell them that the "blue box" and gender stereotypes tell them who they are supposed to be and how they have to behave. Talk to them about how living in the "blue box" is very limiting to them. Ask them what aspects of themselves will fit and won't fit into the "blue box?" How are they going to feel about all this?

- Tell them about the three power types. What type of power does the "blue box" give to our boys? Is it healthy or useful for our boys? Absolutely not. It is only teaching our boys to use their "power over." This type of power won't last.
- Here are some examples of what the "power within" will look like:
  - Embrace your style even if it isn't in fashion
  - Act with integrity (your words and action has to match your morals and values)
  - Express your emotions and vulnerability with courage
  - Resist peer pressure when you know doing something is very wrong
  - Call out people when they use homophobic language
  - Ask for help if you need it
  - Stand up for others or yourself if they or you are being harassed or bullied
  - Doing what you like to do, no matter what others might think.
- Find vulnerable, courageous, and strong men in media. When you are watching television with your child, ask them if the male characters are showing any vulnerability or if they have become slaves of the "blue box? How well has that worked out for them?

- You have to be a great role model. Are you expressing your emotions in healthy ways, or do you keep them bottled up and then explode when the pressure builds up too much? Father's need to have interests and hobbies that aren't completely masculine. Do you normally make comments that reinforce any rule of the "blue box" like "don't cry," "don't be a wimp," "toughen up," or "be a man." You don't have to be hard on yourself but you do need to be honest.

All parents have to work hard to help our boys live their truth and get rid of gender stereotypes. If we can have the courage to talk with our boys, to encourage them to think about gender specific, then we have started off on the right foot. In a world that is perfect, we would be able to do this while looking at the "pink box" and the way they intersect. They do require one another to actually exist. Is this going to be hard? Yes. Is it going to take some time? Yes. Living this way is a lot more interesting than just living in "pink" and "blue."

CHAPTER 9: FATHERS AND SONS

There are no two fathers that are exactly alike. The way the parent is a blend of their strengths and personality, but good fathers have traits that are similar. It's true that fathers do tend to have a closer connection to their sons simple due to the face they understand me, but there are things that a father needs to make sure they do to help their sons grow up into responsible men.

Handle Both Sides

Children need to have structure and nurturance, but it is very easy for couples to split up these jobs instead of both doing both. You shouldn't do this. The father tends to be designated as the drill sergeant type; you son is going to view you as simple intimidating, rigid, and tough. You may be thinking you do what do because you care, but all they see is some guy that is always on edge and nitpicking.

This is the impression they are going to remember, and the one they will likely pass to their sons. Provide your son with more than a one-dimensional view about fatherhood and you. You need to do everything. Be tough when you need to, but be the gentle and nurturing type as well, and work with your partner to do the same.

Help Them Understand The Cave

We've known for a long time that men and women work at problems very differently. Women tend to process things and make sense of problems and emotions by talking about them. Men tend to withdraw into their cave and start mulling things over for what can seem like forever. They work things out in their heads, and then they will eventually come out with what they need to do, and will often skip the backstory of how they got there, which is often frustrating.

If this is how you tend to handle issues, then you should be sensitive to the fact that your son probably won't understand what is going on. He could take your withdrawal and mulling personally, thinking that this action is connected to him, or it can cause him to worry. If you find that you need to withdraw, then let him, along with everybody else in your family, know what's happening. Simply saying, "I'm fine, and this has nothing to do with you, but I need some time to myself to think about some things."

Give Him Your Time

This is about the only thing that you can give and control. Money can easily be lost, but time is only lost if you let it get away. You don't need to worry about the quantity, but, instead, the quality. Stanley Greenspan, a pediatrician and child psychiatrist, came up with what he called Floor Time. This is where you dedicate time each day to spend one-on-one time with your son. This could be 30 minutes, an hour, or just 15 minutes. Let him choose how you will spend this time. You could play some games, wrestle, watch some television, read something, or bake a cake. It simply doesn't matter what you do as long as your son gets your undivided attention, and he gets a bit of time to be in control. This will give you a chance to learn a bit about your son's life. This should be done every day and should never be canceled as a form of punishment. It should be unconditional.

Build Positives

Sure, you may have some things that you want your son to achieve, but he is only going to reach them if you provide him with positives and praise. Make sure he knows how proud you are for the person he is and not for things he does. This might mean counteracting how your father treated you, and try to focus what he did well at in school first, and then discuss the problems. The key word there is to discuss and not scold. Anytime that he shows a seed of being a good person, he is compassionate, proactive, responsible, considerate, make sure he knows. Without providing him feedback, all of his efforts will probably be lost.

Apologize

Men don't do this very well, to begin with. Men are great at being arrogant and blaming their emotions and problems on other people rather than dealing with them. They view apologies as caving in. That's not healthy or conducive for healthy relationships.

Apologize to your son when you overreact. Let him know that you didn't mean to hurt his feelings. This can help to repair your relationships, and it will teach him about humility and responsibility. You are letting him know that he needs to be aware of the impact he has on others, and when things don't go as he had planned it, he should step up and say so.

Show Love

The relationship you have with your partner can help or hinder your son's upbringing, plus, it is probably the only place where he learns what a healthy relationship looks like. You need to show him how to properly handle differences, show respect and affection, and managing emotions. There is no need to be perfect, but you should be proactive. Being calm all the time may not be possible, but you should be sensitive and clear. Take a pass on lectures or speeches. Instead, try to focus on integrity. Do what you say.

This can seem tough, but you have time and room for mistakes. Kids tend to be very forgiving. If you don't know if you are doing well as a dad, take a step back, and look at things. Does your son come to you easily with his problems? Is he comfortable sharing how he feels with you? Does he respect your advice? If he is able to do these things, then you are doing pretty good.

However, if he is dismissing you, pulling away, and afraid to come close, you need to break the pattern. Go to him, even if he tries to pull back at first. Talk, spend time, and give positives. Never underestimate your impact and influence.

CHAPTER 10: MOTHERS AND SONS

That moment you looked into your baby boy's eyes, you knew immediately knew that all the hopes and dreams you had for him rested completely on what you did. Are you going to be able to help him grow into a responsible, confident, and caring man? Every mother is going to question how she is doing while raising her child. If you can follow the below advice, you have a good chance of getting the type of man you want your son to be.

Teach Them Empathy

If a boy is able to know how somebody else is feeling, it will make them a better friend while he is young and a better husband when he gets older. Empathy is a great skill that will help them feel for others and keeps them from doing hurtful things. This is the best foundation that you could give to your son.

Some studies have shown that moms might have a hard time doing this. College students are about 40 percent less empathic than they were when they were younger. There are two possible reasons for this. One is violent video games that numb our brains from other people's pain. The other is social media that is filled with "virtual friends" that our children don't actually know, and they can't create meaningful relationships with.

Things you can do:

- Teach Him to Play What If

Encourage your boy to put himself in another person's shows by using examples from things that he likes, such as sports. When he is watching a football game, sit with him and say things like: "The quarterback seems like he is under a lot of pressure. How would you handle being the quarterback?" It is only going to take a couple of seconds here and there but you are going to be teaching your son to think about the feelings of others and to put himself in their shoes. If you can do this enough through their young years, he will grow into somebody who handles emotional situations extremely well.

- Have Them Read Novels

Studies that were done have shown people who read fiction more than nonfiction will do better when taking empathy tests. Why? The part of the brain that we use to understand the way fictional characters are feeling are the same ones that we use when we try to figure out how others are feeling. When we use these parts of the brain, the stronger our empathy will be.

Make His Sense of Self Stronger

Try to think of a man that you admire. Most of them will have one trait in common, and that is a healthy self-esteem. If a man feels good about himself, this doesn't mean that he is egotistical. It simply means that he feels worthy, competent, and confident. This is what you want your son to be.

Things you can do:

- Stop False Praising Them

When you tell your child that they are the smartest child in the world or that they are the best ball player ever, you are setting expectations that they won't ever be able to live up to. Give them praise for their efforts instead of their talents. Young children will feel accomplished and able to handle any challenge if they get praised for the way they did a task. Say something like: "You worked really hard." When they complete task say: "Great job getting that done." These are a lot better than the normal jargon of "I'm proud of you."

- Stop Labeling Them

Don't ever use the phrase "boys will be boys" or any other phrase that will blame their behavior on their gender. This suggests to them that they can't control their actions. The message our children get from us will play huge roles when developing their self-esteem. If your child hears words that attach them, it will have negative impacts on their self-worth. He is going to believe the things that those phrases imply: "boys are nothing but troublemakers."

CHAPTER 11: HANDLING NEGATIVE EMOTIONS

Children need what is known as emotion coaching. Emotion coaching simply means that you talk to your child about how they are feeling, and then offer them some strategies for a copy with difficult emotions. The goal with this is to make sure you teach, empathize, and reassure.

Many adults, parents included, tend to view a child as a different being that can't experience negative emotions. That they are simply supposed to be happy all the time and that they couldn't possibly know what stress is. In fact, my dad said something similar to me when I was young. I don't remember exactly what I was doing, but I was relaxing somehow and my dad asked why I wasn't doing anything, or something to that effect, and I said I was stressed. Instead of talking to me about that, he said I couldn't be stressed; I was too young to know what it meant.

While kids may be small, they can have some big emotions. Young children will face a lot of frustrations and other reasons to experience negativity. They will face things like fear, anxiety, sadness, and anger.

Kids are a work in progress, and the parts of their brain that control self-regulation is still being developed, so you can't expect your three-year-old son to handle disappointment like a 30-year-old would. They also lack life experiences. They are just learning how emotions work. They aren't as great as reading the intentions and feelings other people.

There are some kids who will have a harder time than others. There are some personality traits that will stay stable over time, and then there are some that place them at a higher risk of emotional issues like depression, anxiety, aggression, or moodiness. This doesn't mean things can't be improved. Children of all ages can learn how to handle their moods; they simply need some help. It's up to you to make sure you provide that help.

So, how do you tend to react when your child is upset? In many cases, parents don't react in a good way. Some parents will dismiss their child's negative emotions. This tells their child that their emotions are unimportant or silly. Other times, parents disapprove of their emotions. They actually notice the emotions of their child, but they view them as offensive. Then there are those parents who do acknowledge and accept their child's negative emotions, but they don't do anything to teach them how to deal.

This last group of parents tends to see things like sadness as something their child has to get over. They may even want to do something more, but they don't what.

All groups of parents mentions, those who dismiss, disapprove, or ignore, aren't necessarily insensitive. They actually probably find it painful to see their child in distress, but they fail to help their child handle those emotional storms. They just sit on the sidelines, or they try to suppress their child's emotions through punishment, threats, or teasing. A common reaction parents have when their child is angry is giving them a time out, even if their child never did anything wrong.

Parents who decide to provide emotion coaching see their child's bad mood as a chance to teach, connect, and empathize. They take the time to see things from their child's view, and then they make sure that their child feels respected and understood. That talk to their child about emotions, and they help their child put their feelings into words. They will also help their child come up with strategies for dealing with negative emotions they experience, and what triggers them.

Destructive Behavior

Sometimes, in the midst of the various emotions your child will display, they can display destructive behavior. Many parents see a child with destructive actions and blame the parent just like there are parents who view a child throwing a temper tantrum in the middle of Wal-Mart and blame the parents for not raising their child right. Those parents are wrong in both cases. Every parent, as long as they are actually involved in raising their child and teaching them about emotions, are doing the best that they can. There are parents out there who simply check out and don't raise their children, and their children have to raise themselves, but that's a different beast. You are reading this, so you are doing the best that you can.

With that out the way, destructive behaviors happen for a reason. These actions are in response to something that is going on in their life that the parent probably isn't aware of. When they act out in a way that they know you won't approve of, it is showing they are feeling disconnected and discomfort. That's the first thing you need to look for. Does your child actually understand what they did is wrong?

Destructive behavior can be small at first, but it can escalate if things aren't addressed. If they do something that was serious and intentional, say scratching up your car with a rock, then their disconnection has grown very large. It may be very angering to see the damage done to your property, but your child is feeling very uncomfortable and is simply displaying this feeling in the only they know how. It is a call for help that you must answer with compassion.

Let's side step for a moment and discuss connection and disconnection. When I say disconnection, I'm not saying that parents aren't spending time with their child, and it definitely doesn't mean that they don't care or love them. It also doesn't mean they are too strict. It simply means that their child doesn't feel accepted or seen.

When a child acts out, they are waving a red flag. Most parents will see this and try to provide their kids what they need. The first thing you need to do is physically stop the behavior if you are witnessing it firsthand. This should come off as easy and comfortable. You are naturally stronger and bigger. Don't go straight to screaming or losing your head. You have to be the calm one in this situation.

Then you need to, ideally, notice what they are doing. It could be that they are hitting, so you could say something lie, "Wow, you feel like hitting. That made you feel like hitting when I did or said that." You need to notice and accept the feelings behind their actions.

Everybody, at some point in their life, feels like pushing the limits or doing something inappropriate. Children feel this more often than adults do. Their cognitive development isn't connected to the maturity of their prefrontal cortex yet, which means they don't have great self-control. This part of their brain will time a long time to develop.

A child needs to feel safe physically, as well as safe in their own feelings. It's also a good idea to think to yourself, "I'm not going to let you..." This will place you in a helpful attitude by helping you to remain calm.

Now, this is easier said than done. It's easy to see the obvious moments of emotional distress, such as your child hitting, but there are trickier ones that can be overlooked. This is very common for kids who become an older sibling. You may focus on making sure he feels understood about how hard it can be to be an older sibling, but they could say things that may not trigger you to think they could be struggling. For example, he could say something like, "I can't tie my own shoes." You know he can, so you simply encourage his independence and to tie his own shoes. However, that statement could be a cry for help. He could be asking you to spend time with him because he is feeling alone.

Then there are common things that we miss because your child's actions seen unreasonable, and we get angry and think they are acting bratty. Every parent experiences this, and there is no shame in it. It's hard to understand why your child pushes away food you made specifically for him or says something crazy like, "I don't want the baby looking at me. These random expressions of emotion are ones we often push back because we don't understand them. It's hard to show empathy towards something we view as angry, mean, or bratty.

Understanding children is a pain in the butt, and we will never be perfect. The best thing we can do is to try out best, and try to put ourselves in their shoes when we think they are outrageous. Hopefully, this will help prevent your child from reaching major destructive actions, but if you wake up one morning to find your child has completely destroyed something important that you, there is a way to handle it that doesn't involve yelling at your child.

You need to look at how you have been viewing and responding to your child because this will dictate your response to the destruction. Take a deep look into your heart. Children become destructive; they are at their worst point, especially if a new sibling has been introduced. Understand that they didn't want to do what they did, but they felt like they had to, and they won't be able to answer the question, "What did you do this?"

Even if you did get angry and lash out initially, take a moment to step back, gather yourself, forgive your kid, and forgive yourself. Peel back your child's layers, and you will be able to figure out why they are acting out. Your conversation with your child could sound like this, "I wish I would have noticed so that I could have stopped you from doing this. It must have been uncomfortable for you to do something that you know would upset us. Yes, we got angry, but understand that we will always, always be here for you and we want to help you not blame you. We will always be on your side."

Recognizing Anxiety and Depression in Children

We've become more and more aware of the issues with depression in children. It's important that we learn how to spot them so that we can intervene and get our children the help they need. Kids get sad from time to time and may act depressed. For many, they will get over the worst in a few days, but some aren't able to.

Parents who are tuned into their child will know deep down when there is something wrong with their kid, and it isn't going away. A kid who gets upset about a friend who treated them unfairly will normally get over this in a few days, but a parent knows when there is something sticking around.

There is no age limit to depression. But, there are two schools of thought on this. Some experts see the depression first and notice that those children end up suffering from anxiety. Then there are others who view anxiety as the underlying issue. But the one thing that they all agree on is the fact that childhood depression is a brain disorder that is caused by chemistry changes in the brain. A lot of the changes will have roots in the hormonal shifts in the teen and young adult years.

Depression in preteens and younger is very rare, but it is still possible. When this happens, it is the environment or the parents. The child has a predisposition, just like a child with a learning disability or autism. It's a blip in their DNA.

Most often than not, depression in pre-puberty children is most often anxiety. This also means that they have a predisposition for developing full-blown depression in adolescents. Anxiety can cause a lot of problems, but it tends to be minimized. Adults tend to view children as these indestructible objects, but they're not.

Childhood anxiety disorders are symptoms that persist and center on a single theme. They create a lot of distress and can disrupt their lives. There are three categories of anxiety disorders.

1. Separation anxiety – This is the most common anxiety disorder for children where they fear there is a threat to their family. They feel like something bad will happen if the family doesn't stay together. On school days, they may experience diarrhea, stomachaches, or headaches. While the symptoms are real, they are caused by their brain and not for a bug.

2. Social phobia – The children are uncomfortable with the social parts of school. They tend to be "socially mute." They talk with their family, but they won't talk to anybody outside of the home and often refuse to go to school.

3. Generalized anxiety disorder – These are the children who worry about the future. They worry about things that probably won't occur for many more years.

You can't just hope that they will grow out of it. These experiences cause them to feel hopeless, and hopelessness is only going to make them want to hurt themselves. There are some common signs to look out for that mean your child could be depressed:

- Expressions or thoughts of self-destructive behavior or suicide
- Efforts or talks of running away
- A major changing in sleeping or eating habits
- Poor concentration
- Poor performance or frequent absences in school
- Frequent complaints of illnesses like stomachaches or headaches
- Difficulty with relationships
- Increased hostility, anger, or irritability
- Extreme sensitivity to failure or rejection
- Guilt and low self-esteem
- Poor communication and social isolation
- Low energy or persistent boredom
- Decreased interest in activities or unable to enjoy what they used to like doing
- Hopelessness
- Frequent crying, tearfulness, or sadness

If you notice several of these symptoms in your child, you may want to reach out to a mental health care provider that specializes in children. Your child's regular doctor may not be able to help you with the diagnosis, but they could possibly point you in the right direction. Treatment will require some help on the parents part as well.

Antidepressants may be prescribed, but should not and cannot be the only source of treatment.

Unfortunately, a lot of children will have really good reasons to be depressed and sad. These children don't have depression, though they suffer from demoralization. Children who live in poverty, have neglectful or abusive parents, divorced and fighting parents, or inadequate education often become demoralized. These situations don't cause depression; instead, they cause behavioral symptoms. These kids tend to be tearful, unhappy, and rambunctious. People should feel bad when they are living a crummy life.

It's not just underprivileged that can cause demoralization. A lot of what appears to be depression is the byproduct of overscheduled, over-pressured families and youth. When you cut things back and take the pressure off your children, the symptoms will start to go away.

CHAPTER 12: MEDIA AND THE BOYS' MIND

Teenagers are normally pretty smart about media messages. They don't take to heart everything they see on social or other types of media. You, as a parent, could help to create the skills they need when dealing with media influence.

The influence that media has on teenagers could be direct and deliberate. Advertising is normally directed at teenagers and children. This means that they are very conscious of images and brands.

The influence that media has could be indirect. It could include sexualized content and images on YouTube, Facebook, Snapchat, or Instagram. It could include violent images, vulgar language in songs, video games, documentaries, and news outlets. This type of media could suggest to teenagers that specific behaviors and looks are normal.

Positive Influences

There is some good news. Social and other types of media could have positive influences on a teenager's attitude and behavior.

- Identity

There are some good quality shows on television as well as some movies that could help a teenager explore their identity, such as ethics, gender, relationships, or sexuality. The way they treat ethics in shows such as *The Good Place*, gender as in *Ride Like a Girl*, or sexuality in movies like *Bohemian Rhapsody*, can do a lot for a young child. If you watch these shows with your child, it is a wonderful time to have a discussion with them.

- Lifestyle and Health

Teenagers can pick up important health messages from social and other types of media. These could include messages that try to prevent youth suicide and depression, encourages a healthy lifestyle and eating habits, or promotes respectful, positive relationships.

- Citizenship

Teenagers that take an interest in the news will be interested in political and major social problems such as climate change. Media could encourage them to get involved in their communities.

Experts haven't been able to agree on whether video game violence could cause violence or aggression in a teenager's life. They have agreed that the only way to handle the problem of violence in video games is by talking to them about it and sharing your family's values.

Negative Influences

Media messages could have unhealthy or negative influences on a teenager's attitude and behavior in areas such as citizenship, health, and body image.

- Citizenship

In order for a teenager to be a responsible citizen, they need good-quality and reliable information. Social and other media could be used negatively during elections or other times. "Fake news" could influence a teenager to believe false information about a celebrity, public figure, or politician. There might be times when online forums will promote hateful or biased attitudes towards people or groups of individuals.

- Lifestyle and Health

Social or other media could influence a teenager's decision about their lifestyle and health. Media content and messages might make it look normal, grown up or cool to take drugs, drink alcohol, smoke or eat junk food.

- Body Image

Any child's body image could be influenced by advertising, other media outlets, and social media. If a teenager is exposed to unrealistic muscly or thin body types enough, they will follow it. This can have an impact on their dieting behaviors and body image. This is very true if there isn't anyone to disagree with the messages they see like: "this is beautiful."

You need to remember that bad or good media is only one of many influences on a teenager's attitude and behavior. Other influences might include cultural background, peers, friends, family, and many others. Most of these influences are a lot more powerful than any media influence.

Celebrity Influences

Celebrities and how they use social media could be a powerful influence on teenagers. Basically, teenagers are attracted to behaviors, products, or lifestyles that celebrities show on social media. This might be negative influences like Logan Paul's risky behaviors on YouTube. There are many celebrities whose behaviors, values, and lifestyles will give your teenager positive examples like Elise Ecklund's YouTube channel.

Teenagers and children have to be careful that there are some celebrities get paid to advertise products that they endorse.

Handling Media's Influence

Being exposed to social media's messages is just another part of life today, but you could help your child find the things that they should pay attention to.

- Encourage Questions

When you talk to your child about social media, you could encourage them to ask questions. This can give them a chance to find the difference between opinion and facts, understand bias, identify advertising, and be aware of them misusing statistics.

You can find one Instagram or YouTube channel that your child follows and ask them:

- Why do they want you to feel this way?
- How does this make you feel?
- What do they want from you?
- What is their motivation?
- Who is behind all this?

You can do this for celebrities. Have your child ask themselves:

- How do they make you feel about yourself?
- What values do they have?
- Are they really like this in real life?
- Do they present themselves realistically?
- Why do you like them?

During election times, share some political memes with your child. Have your child ask:

- How does this meme influence a voter?
- Who created this meme?
- Why did they create this meme?
- What ideas are they promoting?

Talk about Media Messages

The best way that you can help your child get through social media's influence is to talk to them about the messages that the media is sending. If your child likes to watch tech channels on YouTube, you might talk to them about sponsorship and advertising.

If your child likes video games such as Grand Theft Auto, you could talk about criminal activity, exploiting women, and violence. You might talk to them about who they would handle these types of situations if they were faced with them in real life.

If your child likes to spend time watching forums, it is perfectly fine to ask what the people talk about on that particular forum. You could ask if the forum supports specific attitudes towards sexuality, gender, ethnicity, or race or if any of their attitudes are hateful or biased.

Understanding Advertising

You could help limit the amount of influence that advertising has on your child by talking about the way advertising sells products and ideas. You might encourage your child to ask:

- What messages did the advertiser send about what men, women, boys, and girls need to drink, eat, do, wear, or look like?
- How do you feel about the product?
- Did their advertising like their product with a certain type of lifestyle?

Balancing Social Media's Influence

If your child can balance social media with other things like creative and physical activities and being with their friends face to face, they will be in contact with many different influences. These might include media, family, mentors, community, and peers.

You could introduce your child to positive, real life models, too. You can do this by joining mentoring programs, sporting clubs, or local community groups.

You are still the most important role model for your child. If you are questioning and informed consumer, you can show your child ways to handle media influences. Some of this could be ignoring advertisements for the next new gadget. You could talk to your child about why they follow specific people on Instagram or Twitter.

CHAPTER 13: HELPING THE BOYS' HEART, MIND, AND BODY

The one thing parents want is to raise their son right. What right means to you will likely be different from what another parent believes. In order to make sure your son does grow up to be a great person, you have to look out for all of him. You want to make sure his heart, mind, and body are all healthy.

Now, our culture can have a very different view on how to raise a boy to be a man. These cultural influences can affect how you interact with your son, the way he acts with others, and how he feels inside.

Society says boys have to be confident and strong. This means that society believes boys shouldn't be needy, sensitive, or emotional. This teaches boys that "masculine" emotions, like aggression and anger, are okay, but other emotions, like fear, have to be silenced and hidden. And all of those "feminine traits" have to be stored up and never shared.

Reinforcing these beliefs only hurt your son. Not being able to share how they really feel will have a detrimental effect on their mind. That's why if you sense that something is bothering your son, spend some time with him to try to get him to share with you what is bothering him. Always be respectful of his feelings.

Another issue is disciplining. Boys and girls handle harsh discipline in very different ways. There is a very common correlation between harsh discipline and physical misbehavior. Since boys tend to be more physical and active, they tend to face more severe discipline. Couple this with the fact that many parents feel they have to "toughen up" their sons, which will cause them to use intimidation, fear, and power tactics.

While it may seem like these tactics work, the success is actually short-term and tends to backfire. Boys subjected to this form of discipline tend to make decisions based on external factors, which means what their teachers and parents expect. They never learn how to use their internal compass.

Kids view their parents as larger than life. When they do something you don't like, and you act out angrily, they don't necessarily get the message you were trying to convey. You are trying to teach them a lesson of not to do that while yelling, but all they see the emotional nuances of the moment. They are going to remember the power of your anger, how he felt, and where he was. Most parents aren't going to want their child to remember the anger. Instead, they would rather them remember the lesson.

If you have been using fear and anger as disciplinary tactics, just remember that your son is going to remember the fury and not the reason why you were upset.

10 Tips For Raising an All Around Healthy Son

1. Praise his positives

"Boy" actions, even if they are age-appropriate, tend to be difficult to deal with. Boys are faced with a lot of scolding, reprimanding, and correcting at home and in school. Parents of girls will often complain boys get the most attention in classes, but a lot of that attention tends to be negative. This means that whenever possible, you need to catch your son "being good." Make sure that he knows that you appreciate his efforts in channeling his energy into something that is rewarding and constructive.

2. Help out at school

Speak with your son's teacher on a regular basis to find out where his weaknesses and strengths are in class. Let them know, as well, what you believe his strengths are. Check his homework, but do it for him, and encourage to him listen or read a story every day.

3. Encourage all interests whether they are "boy" activities or not

If your son is interested in dance, he may face teasing, but you should let him. You will need to instill a strong sense of self and encourage him to accept the differences in people. This will help him to deal with teasing that he might face. So, if he says he wants to take ballet, sign him up. Besides, next year he could want to join the baseball team.

4.   Make sure he has music in his life

Letting him learn an instrument can give him a valuable sense of accomplishment. There are studies that suggest music lessons can help to improve children's memory and thinking skills. If your son prefers group activities, then he could try out a children's chorus or school band. With group activities, you won't face as much practice time at home since they practice together a lot. You can also take him to musical theater or concerts.

5.   Give him a chance to use social skills

A lot of boys don't create close intimate friendships as girls can. They tend to play in groups and fight for leadership. Help to strengthen his one-on-one connections by creating playdates, encourage sharing, using his manners, and playing nice.

6.   Don't worry about his masculinity

Even the toughest guy out there tends to have a soft side, at least the good ones do. A boy who likes cuddling with stuffed animals is developing a skill that is going to help him as an adult.

7. Don't try to control his engine

Boys often have a lot of energy, which will become pent-up if he isn't allowed to blow off some steam. The important thing is to make sure your son knows the time and place where he should and should not go full steam ahead.

8. Provide him with physical affection

Studies have found that parents don't have as much physical contact with boys as they do with girls, which is something that starts in toddlerhood. Girls aren't the only ones that need cuddles. Getting hugs from their parents help your son to feel secure and safe.

As boys age, they tend to shy away from kisses and hugs, especially if their friends are around. Even if they express not wanting the attention, they still need affection. This means that you may need to provide your son with hugs and touches in a sneaky way. Rubbing his back while he is helping in the kitchen or a quick hug when nobody is looking helps.

9. Allow him to show all of his emotions

We've already said what society thinks boys should do, so it's up to you to teach them society is wrong that he can express any emotion that he is feeling. He'll get upset from time to time; let him express that, as long as he isn't hurting himself or anything. Once he has regained control, sit him down and talk about what he was feeling.

10. Give him responsibility

Finishing tasks and following directions are skills that boys develop more slowly. Practice will help them. Start asking them as a preschooler to bring you a spoon to stir the pancake batter. Have your grade-school take care of the family pet. Giving him a sense of responsibility will help him in school, and the home will run more smoothly as well.

CHAPTER 14: ENCOURAGEMENT AND COMPETITION

If competition is done correctly, it can help your child learn some skills that they will use during their lives. Some parents might look at competition as being a dirty word because it puts too much pressure on children to try to be their best. They will argue, but it could place unnecessary stress and cause children to feel disappointed if they don't feel like they measure up to the other children. To keep your child away from disappointment, many parents will either say that everybody is a winner or completely stay away from situations that are competitive.

Is having a shelf full of participation trophies the right answer? Not really. Experts in child development point out that healthy competition can actually be good for children. It can set them up for losses and winds later on in their life. They aren't always going to get that promotion. Activities that are competitive could help them develop the right skills they will use in their adulthood, such as tenacity, empathy, and taking turns.

Competitions could help children learn that it isn't always the smartest or best people who are successful but the ones who work hard. Children who take part in competitions will earn crucial social skills by interacting with others while learning that hard work is valuable while developing self-efficacy and self-esteem.

Competitions are a healthy setting to help your child learn ways to be a team player. Most games that are cooperative can teach your child to solve problems by being part of a team. This helps them learn skills by finding the common good within a group.

The main thing to make sure of is that this atmosphere needs to promote constructive competition. This isn't always something that your child will be able to figure out or talk to you about, so notice how they react when in a competitive situation.

If your child is involved in competitions that are healthy, they might:

- Show signs of better self-esteem
- Want to better themselves because they learned new skills
- Learned how to lose and win gracefully
- Ask to do the activity again

If your child is involved in a competition that isn't healthy, they might:

- Be showing signs of loss of appetite, problems sleeping, anxiety, or depression. These are all red flags that need to be discussed. Children who are competitive might show signs of anxiety right before a test or game but they shouldn't be worried constantly so that it begins affecting other aspects of their lives.
- Tell you they don't want to play
- Fake being sick to stay away
- Resist participating in the activity

Encouraging Healthy Competition

Falling short of winning the top prize or losing a close game isn't ever easy for anybody, but you can help your child think about competition in a positive manner. It can help define accomplishments not as just a winning an activity, but by setting goals for anything they decide to do and actually accomplish. You should try to be there to support your child through any challenge and reinforce a message that it is fine to lose as long as they give it their best and learn from their experience. You have to model good behavior. This is a powerful tool. You can't blame the referees after the game is over.

Don't ever underestimate the perspective of change. The best part of participating in healthy competitions is that children learn that the most important competitor is themself. I had a friend whose five year old like participating in cross country running competitions. Their son repeatedly lost but rather than concentrating on his losses, they focused on him beating his time.

They taught him not to worry about how fast all the other children were but just learn to race against the clock. They set times for him to do at a specific distance. This caused his perspective to change from competing against the other children to just competing against his own time. Because of this, he stopped experiencing failures to experiencing success every time he beat his time. He continued enjoying cross country even though he was usually the last child over the finish line.

Encouraging Your Child

It can be very hard to motivate a child. As a parent, we normally have inaccurate and funny beliefs that our children don't care if we don't' twist their arms. The truth is that when you attempt to motivate your child, it is actually working against you.

There is no way to make your child care about something just because you do. You could be getting in their way. Because of all the push and pull when trying to motivate your child will normally just turn into a power struggle. There is something very wrong if you care more than your child does.

If you have been getting all up in your child's business and try to make them care just because you care, it is important for you to stop and ask this question: "What is my child's responsibility here? What is mine?" If your child isn't doing his homework, your job is to hold them accountable and show them how the world works. Out in the big world, if you don't do your work, you aren't going to get a paycheck.

Give your child some consequences to show them what will happen from his poor choices. Don't confuse the reason why you are doing this by thinking that you will make them care about his homework just because you care. Consequences are put into place to create motivation. They are given because you are a parent. Basically, you can't motivate anybody else to care. Your role is to influence and inspire.

Because we are parents, we usually feel responsible for how our child turns out in life. Know what this isn't ever the case because your child is the only one responsible for their own choices. Since we think that our child's success is all dependent on us, we go into a place where we seriously don't belong. We have been taught that we have to control our children so we jump in their box without even thinking about it. We think we have to motivate our children to want specific things out of life. This will only cause them to function because of your reaction.

Your child will probably comply just to get you off their back of just to please you; this doesn't help their self-motivation. You need to influence and inspire your children. Everyone wants their child to be motivated. It's the way we get them there that makes a difference.

Some children are as motivated as others. Some children are smart as can be, but they constantly bring home report cards that have Ds and Fs on it. Some just sit in their desks at school gazing out into space in spite of their teacher's efforts. Your child might forget their homework or just forgets to turn them in. You might have a teenager who isn't interested in anything and doesn't have any passion or hobbies. They might just give up too easy or just don't want to try. Even with all your efforts, they stay stuck or begin falling behind. If you have other concerns, check with your child's doctor or school to see if they have learning problems, addictions, depression, ADHD, or other conditions.

If your child still isn't motivated, it can create a lot of frustration and worry that might lead to despair. This is where the trouble begins. The trouble here is your reaction to the child's lack of motivation. If you feel nervous for them, you might try to motivate them out of your own anxiety, and this will make you forget that it isn't possible to make anyone care.

You need to ask yourself these questions:

- Does your fear make you continue to try to get them to be more motivated?

- Does feeling helpless make you begin fighting with your partner sho doesn't seem to do as much as you do to get your child motivated?

- When you get frustrated, do you punish, beg, scream, yell, or throw your hands up in defeat?

- Does your worrying cause you to over function, cajole, push, hover, or nag your child?

If you see yourself do any of the above, you have seen your child resist. They have asked you to get off their backs. They might have started rebelling or digging in their heels more. Understand this: it doesn't matter if they fight you or do what you want; the result is going to be that they aren't going to be any more motivated than they were before. They might eventually do what you want them to, but your goal of getting them to be self-motivated is a long way off.

How You Can Inspire Your Child to Get Motivated

1. Never allow your anxiety to push them to be motivated. You are only motivating them to resist you. They will only comply to get you to calm down. They only want you to leave them alone. This isn't going to motivate them. It is only teaching them to resist and appease you. It will te become about reacting to you rather than focusing and finding their own internal

motivation. Your need and anxiety will only cause a power struggle between the two of you.

2. You have to be inspiring. The best way to motivate your child is to stop motivating them. You should work to inspire your child instead. How can you do this? You have to be inspiring. You can ask yourself if how you are behaving is controlling or inspiring. You have to realize that your child is going to run away if you control them too much. Think about somebody who inspires you and work for that goal. The only thing that you are going to motivate if you push your child is their motivation to resist you.

3. Allow them to make their own choices and let them face the consequences of those choices. If it is a poor choice, hold them accountable by allowing them to face the consequences that follow it. If you set a consequence of taking their computer away if they don't' do their homework, put their need for using the computer in their hands. If they finish their work, they get computer time. This will be the motivation for them to do the right thing without having to tell them what they need to do, how they need to do it, and telling them why they should care. Being a parent, you have to ask yourself: "What will I put up with? What are my principles and values?" Then you need to stick with them.

4. You need to ask yourself some questions:

a. What are my childs ambitions and goals?

b. What questions could I ask them to help them find and explore their interests?

c. What does my child really want?

d. What will motivate my child?

You need to step away until you can see your child as their own person. Then just observe. Talk to them until you can answer the above questions. After that, just listen to them. Don't listen for what you would like the answer to be but to what they said. Just learn to listen. Respect their answers, especially if you don't agree.

5. Pick the door you would like to go into. Visualize two different doors. The first door is for a parent that wants to motivate their child to do the right things in their life such as: getting up, going to school, doing their work, and being successful. The second door is for the parent that wants their child to be self-motivated and do these things by themselves. They would like to influence their child to work for what they are interested in. They want them to not just do the right things but to actually want to do the right things.

Which door are you going to enter? If you go through the first door, the only way you are going to achieve the goal is to cajole, reward, bribe, nag, beg, punish, and push. If you pick the second door, then you are going to achieve the goal by asking various questions. Instead of saying: "Did you do your homework?" you are going to say: "Why did you do your homework today rather than yesterday? I say that you did your geometry yesterday and your history today. What is the difference?" You need to turn into an investigator, explore, uncover, and help your child find their own motivation.

6. It isn't your fault. You have to understand that your child lacking motivation isn't your fault. You can't personalize it. If you do this, you might contribute to their underachieving by causing more resistance.

Look at it like this. If you get too close to a mirror, you don't see yourself; you just become a blur. When you step back, you can see yourself better. Do this with your child. There are times when we are just too close. We become so enmeshed with their lives that we can't see them as being separate from us. If we stand back enough, you can begin to see your child as their own person and begin figuring out what makes them tick. Then you will begin to understand them, too. Once you can step back and just watch, you will know what works for them, why he is reaching to specific thins and what gets them motivated. There are going to be things that he isn't going to be motivated about but still has to do them. He might hate doing chores and will try to get out of them, and this is when you give out consequences.

Your goal is to influence your child when they have to do things they don't want to do. You have to get to know them well enough to figure out their desires. You need to strengthen their skills so they can define what is important to them. You need to help your child find out who they are but let them do it by themselves. They need to find out what is important to them and what they need to do to make these things happen. Your responsibility is helping them do that not doing it for them. You have to stay out of their way so they can find out what they are, where their own interests are, and what they are thinking.

CHAPTER 15: TURNING MISTAKES INTO SUCCESS

I think everybody can relate to this. Growing up, I was amazed by other kids, and even adults, who seemed to have the raw talent for music, academics, sports, and other things. I felt that only this innate, effortless talent was the only way to succeed. My mom did her best to influence and encourage me by using the overused phrase, "If at first you don't succeed, try, try again."

I was always trying new things, but I would give up if I didn't do well instantly. It wasn't until much later that I learn making mistakes is a healthy part of learning, and it helps provide you with the best opportunities for success.

This is why it is so important to make sure your child understands that mistakes don't mean failure. Instead, they are a route to success. We are going to go over three ways to do this.

Reframe Their Perspective of Mistakes

For the most part, kids view mistakes as they "did something wrong." This outlook makes it pretty hard to face a challenge.

People who adopt this type of mindset, meaning they believe that creative ability, intelligence, and character are immutable and innate, end up capping their own potential by staying away from possible challenges.

Those who believe that abilities and intelligence are assets that can be cultivated and nurtured through hard work have a "growth mindset." For children who have this mindset, they see mistakes as a learning opportunity. Children who have a growth mindset will take on challenges, bounce back from mistakes, and thrive academically.

Parents can help give their kids a growth mindset. For example, simply realizing the fact that the brain is a muscle that can be developed will help you do that. Let your child have space to work out their problems, and to make mistakes without worrying about punishment, shame, or judgment can also help cultivate a growth mindset.

Change How You React to Their Mistakes

A lot of us learned early on to try and hide our mistakes, trying to add is much space between us and the failure as we can. While society, and human nature in general, are to blame for reinforcing this, parents have the power to break this thinking pattern.

If children are afraid of the consequences of accidentally knocking a plant over, getting a bad grade, or cutting their sister's band, we are teaching to fear to make mistakes. This will include the important mistakes that they have to make to grow into well-functioning adults. While this does not mean there shouldn't be any consequences, it does mean that you need to look at how you react, as parents, to mistakes your children make. Most mistakes kids make are harmless. Most of them are going to have fixable outcomes that a child can learn from.

Mistakes play a part in trying and practicing, which are two things that you need to encourage your children to do at all times. By reacting calmly to mistakes, you can establish a healthy mentality in your child, and with consistent application, you can make it stick.

Help Them Stop Negative Self-Talk

It is very common to cultivate self-criticism after you make a mistake. When your child makes a mistake, this is a time to teach them how to treat themselves like they would treat a best friend. Research has found that self-compassion is better than self-criticism when it comes to reaching our goals.

But you may be asking, shouldn't we be teaching taking responsibility for our mistakes. Dr. Kristin Neff, a self-compassion pioneer, says there are some common misconceptions when it comes to self-compassion.

First, self-compassion isn't the same as self-pity. Self-pity lands closer to being self-absorbed. It ignores that lots of other people have experienced the same thing, and focuses on what took place and not what should happen now.

Second, self-compassion does not equate self-indulgence. When you teach a child self-compassion, it doesn't mean you coddle them or teach them how to coddle themselves. Teach your child that being self-compassionate involves setting themselves up for success and growth. Self-indulgence tends to involve short-term pleasure, which is normally not all that compassionate.

Third, self-compassion and self-esteem are not the same. In our culture, value is placed on being special and standing out. This causes the average person to believe they need to be above average, which makes self-esteem depending on figuring out your value. Self-compassion, on the other hand, is blind to value. With compassion, you know you are enough right now.

It is important that we teach children to feel compassion for themselves for the simple fact that they are human. Self-compassion gives kids a chance to acknowledge, observe, and learn from mistakes while not feeling shame.

If you teach your child to see mistakes as opportunities, embrace them, and practice self-compassion, you will be providing them with exponential and powerful rewarding gifts.

CHAPTER 16: LEARN FROM FAILURE

Parents like to think their mission is helping their children succeed. There is a growing realization with teachers and other professionals that work with children that children need help learning ways to fail.

When they don't learn how to be vulnerable, it leaves them vulnerable to developing anxiety. It can lead to meltdowns when they finally fail. It doesn't matter if it happens in college or preschool. What is even more important, it could cause children to stop trying or stop trying new things.

This is why one of the greatest athletes in the world, Michael Jordan, spent years preaching how important it is to lose. Jordan spoke extensively about how resilience and perseverance when faced with challenges both off and on the court, is what made him the winner he became.

The bad news is that the world puts a lot of pressure on children to be better than everyone else. We, as parents, are compelled to help them in all ways possible. Children are becoming more and more distraught over the smallest mistake.

A friend's son began taking piano lessons at the age of six. Anytime he would play a wrong note, he would take the music book and smack himself over the head with it. His music teacher said that she hadn't ever seen a child who was hard on himself. To help him out, she told him that if he did make a mistake, he needed to treat himself the same way that he would treat his younger brother. Nobody will be able to learn if people are being mean to them. This is why he couldn't be mean to himself.

Another friend's daughter became very upset when she didn't get into a high school that her other friends got into. She started to harm herself. She remembers hearing her say that the disappointment and pressure was horrible.

Frustration and distress tolerance is a life skill that is important to master. When talking about school, they need to be able to tolerate imperfection. Building this skill is needed for children to be able to be independent and succeed in their future endeavors. These might be academic goals, personal goals, or just figuring out ways to deal with others.

How can parents teach children how to fail? We have done this multistep process:

- Show Empathy

You have to empathize with your child. Realize that they are in distress. Don't just tell them that it will be okay, or they will do better the next time. This invalidates their feelings of disappointment and frustration. You, as a parent, should change your language: "I can see that you are really disappointed; I know you really want to do better."

- Be a Model

Explain to them that failure is just another part of life and that it happens to everybody. Let them know that you have even failed. You can even share some examples of ways that you have failed. We can model ways to handle their disappointment, like losing a promotion at work. Children aren't exposed to the realities of life like failures, missteps, and mistakes. Everyone likes things to go according to their plans; it is important that we teach children that it is fine if they don't.

- Teachable Moments

Any time your child fails, it becomes a chance for a parent to teach skills like problem solving and acceptance. Your child and you could try to figure out what they can do the next time to help them succeed. Maybe they could study a different way to talk with their teacher about problems they might be having.

It becomes a balance of change and acceptance. It is all about accepting the situation for what it is and creating tolerance for frustration while asking: "Can we change things in the future. Are we able to learn from this?"

- Let Your Child Fail

It is extremely hard to watch your child fall but they will only learn ways to handle disappointment through trial and error. Parents have to stop hovering. If we don't, we are going to rob them of experiences that use problem solving skills that will set them on a path of being confident and resilient in order to take on new challenges.

- Therapy

If your child is having a hard time functioning because they are scared to fail, they might need therapy. If your child hasn't been diagnosed with an anxiety disorder, she still might be frozen with anxiety. If this happens, it is called exposure therapy. We have to expose them slowly to things that are not perfect.

As parents, we will complain that homework is taking too long because your child is so stressed that they are going to constantly rip it up and begin again. We need to teach our children that it is fine to spell a word wrong and continue going forward. In therapy, their therapist might have them write something and tell them to make mistakes like using bad handwriting so that they get used to doing something wrong isn't the end of the world.

They will tell the child that they are going to practice making mistakes. They understand that it is uncomfortable and that with practice, the child will learn ways to tolerate it. There are several ways parents can help their children move past their failures.

Failing is painful for children. But they can only succeed if they can learn the skills needed to handle anything life that throws at them.

CHAPTER 17: UNIVERSITY AND COLLEGE

The things that students have to send to colleges show them a lot about their academic readiness while they are at home with supportive high school teachers, friends, and family, but that's about it. It doesn't help tell them about their psychological readiness, maturity, or emotional readiness. College applications don't let you know if your child is fully ready for college.

College admissions committees really don't have a good track record. About 58% of all college freshmen returned for their sophomore year. There are quite a few freshmen who completed applications that said they were ready, but they weren't.

For parents, it's very easy to lose sight of your goals. Every parent envisions their child's future. They go to college, get married, have kids, and so on. But it isn't simply the act of going to college that parents want; instead, it's thriving in college that parents want. To reach that goal, you have to make sure your son start college when they are ready, and not when all of their classmates are ready. For most parents, your son has been dropping hints about their readiness all through high school. So, to make sure that your son is ready for college or university, let's look at some questions.

Who is Applying?

If you find yourself dragging your son through the college application process, that should be a big red flag. When a parent is managing their child's college application and pulling their resistant or passive teen through it, they need to take a look on if their child is going to do well in college the next year.

As soon as your child starts high school, or at least by their sophomore year, you need to start talking to them about college. This doesn't mean asking them what college they want to go to, but if college interests them. Once the application process starts, teens should feel that the next step is their decision.

Can He Cope with "Hard" Feelings?

A teen's emotional life is full of turmoil. In high school, as well as college, kids will face romantic, social, and academic setbacks. They will see times of exuberance and triumph, and times of disappointment and doubt. This is very normal and desirable so that your teen is prepared for adult life.

Looking at how your teen deals with the challenging times will shed some light on how ready they are for life on their own. If they do bad on a test, do they go for a run, or do they start snacking a lot? If a love interest turns them down, do they listen to music or turn to something illegal? If they are facing doubt, do they call you to look for a compassionate listener or someone to solve their issues? Are they able to handle things without help for you? Students who tend to struggle with dealing with this independently in high school will likely feel overwhelmed in college.

Does Your Teen Have Self-Care Down?

Self-care is one of the most basic requirements when it comes to college. This covers a large area of issues from eating to sleep to self-control to exercise, and it is important that you look at how your teen manages these things without your pushing. Teens you have to remind to go to bed, who don't understand the nutritional needs they have, or find it hard to show self-control in the presence of distractions, will likely struggle on their own.

This self-care also requires your teen to be able to manage money, talk with authority figures or teachers, make travel arrangements, and make doctor's appointments.

Are They Able to Manage Their Time?

In theory, high schoolers should be given more control over their time and learn how to handle it, but in reality, they have a very structured life. When they start college, they will have more free time and flexibility, and managing their time becomes something new for them.

The maturity needed for this depends on their brain development, but teens who show in high school that they often struggle to turn their work in on time or find it hard managing the competing demands of all of their classes and long-term assignments will likely find college challenging. Parents who intervene all the time with reminders will often fail to realize their child can't manage their time.

Do They Know How To and When To Seek Help?

It's been your job for a long time to take them to the doctor when you feel like they need to, or suggest that they should talk to their teacher for extra help. Once they are off at college, they are going to have to decide for themselves if they need to find help of some type. Teens that haven't learn how to assess the problems and find appropriate help can falter when they face a problem.

Is Your Teen Able to Assess Risk?

College will present them with more risky behaviors. Students in college have to constantly assess the risks of what they do. If your teen is already making poor decisions when it comes to alcohol, drugs, or sex, are they going to be able to think through all of the implications of what they are doing? Kids who think through risk properly have moved from "What are the odds I will get caught?" to "What could go wrong if I do this?"

Is Your Teen Struggling With Key Academics?

Your child could be doing fairly well overall, but they may be struggling in certain academic areas that are important for college success, such as essay-writing, math skills, basic algebra, problem-solving, and analyzing literature. Parents have to look over their child's report card, but it also doesn't hurt to look over their child's homework to see if there is anything that they may be struggling with.

College is a very expensive gift, so it's important to know if your child is ready and will appreciate it. While, in the US, it isn't normal for a student to take a gap year, there are a lot of experts who say that taking a year off from studies can be very mature for your teen. Most colleges will allow students to defer for a year.

CHAPTER 18: KEEPING HOPE FOR THE FUTURE

Eventually, your child is going to leave home, and this can be the hardest part of your son's life, not for him, but for you. The most important thing is to make sure your son feels ready, and if you feel that he is ready, then it may just help some of the pain of your child leaving home.

Empty nest syndrome is very real. But this is what you have been preparing your child for, isn't it?

I mentioned the idea of a gap year. As your high school senior is working through their applications to college, you may want to bring up the idea of a gap year to see if they feel that would help them prepare more for college and their future. This is a 12 month period where they can spend their time traveling, working, or exploring possible career directions.

Studies have been done that found that those who took a year off before college were more confident. One student who took a gap year said that she could spot the students who hadn't taken a year off before they started school. It helps to make them more confident about being away from home. They understand why they are in college and don't feel like they are doing it simply because their parents have told them to. They also understand what they want to accomplish. They are less likely to fritter away their college years partying and drinking. The most important thing for gap-year students was to have skills and a career direction by the end of school.

Let your child know all of these things about a gap year. Too many parents worry that their child won't go onto college if they take a gap year, but most do. They can also spend their gap year interning, which will look good on future job applications, and can help them decide what they may want to major in.

They may even get a job that they absolutely despise, which can help them know that they want to have a degree to make sure that they can get a job that they like.

Besides talking to them about this gap year and college, take the time to make sure your child knows the essentials, like cooking, laundry, balancing a checkbook, and so on, to help reduce your worries about how they will fare. Also, and this is simply for you, you can also look at new projects and other assignments at work. Staying busy can help to soften your sadness, and it will help you find purpose.

It's also important that you keep things positive for yourself and your child. Help each other see this new transition as a big adventure. Provide them with some space to figure out things on their own. You can mark this transition with some type of ritual. This could be planting a tree to help commemorate this moment as a new beginning and a rite of passage.

These next few things we will talk about are solely for parents. Children will likely be ready to move out, although once they get on their own, they may have a different view of things until they get used to it, parents are never really ready. In order to make sure that your child stays confident in their future, it is important that you remain as calm as you can. You don't want your teen to think you are getting emotional and upset because you are worried that they won't make, do you?

- Be gentle with yourself

You are losing somebody with this transition. Maybe not permanently, but it is still a loss, so experiencing things like anxiety, loneliness, and sadness is common. There isn't one best way to handle this change. You could be wondering if you have just lost your purpose, or you could be feeling intense grief. You may also experience concern for your child's safety when it comes to thoughts of them traversing the adult world. This completely normal and justified and it is going to pass with time. A good way to handle all of these emotions is to write things down in a journal or talk to your partner. They are likely feeling the same thing.

- Self-care and passion projects can help

As you get your child ready to leave home, whether this is getting packed up for college or going through a checklist of stuff that they are going to need for their first job, it is going to be crazy. So, make sure that you plan out some personal time for yourself. Take a walk outdoors, take a nap, or go to your favorite exercise class. Making sure your rest and perform some soothing self-care routines can help to mitigate any loss you may be feeling.

- Understand that letting go is a process

Your child is going to become an independent adult through a slow process that is going to happen over time. While this moment is an ending, it also marks the beginning of something new and exciting for you and your child. You aren't going to lose touch with them; you just don't have to pick up their shoes anymore. With today's technology, you can easily stay connected through email, text, calling, or even through an old fashioned letter.

- Find some support

You and your partner should lean into each other during this time, but you can also turn to people outside the home to see how others dealt with this change. It is also easy to end up losing contact with friends you made through your child. Build your own community with them, or others, and reach out. Go out and participate in things that you may not have thought about or been able to do as a parent.

- View this time as a time for growth

You have to let go of a sweet time, the time that you spend with your child at home. But remember, every coin has two sides, and the right openness, perspective, and attitude, this can be a point of amazing growth. In fact, there is some research that has suggested parents enjoy the freedom and a better connection with their spouse that an empty nest can give them.

You could discover that you have rekindled a flame in your marriage because you have more time to spend with the one you love. You are also going to have more time for travel, hobbies, goals, and other interests. You will have the chance to create a different relationship with your adult child. Since they can make their own decisions, and they will start to see you as a loyal mentor, friend, and confidant.

CONCLUSION

Thank you for making it through to the end of *Bringing Up Boys*, let's hope it was informative and able to provide you with all of the tools you need to achieve your goals whatever they may be.

The next step is to start using the information you have learned. Everybody is different, and that includes children, so you will have to figure out what works best for your son. The most important thing is to make sure that you spend time with him, whether you are his mother or father. Do things together and make sure that he actually likes doing them. Forcing him to do things he doesn't like is only going to negative feelings and push you two apart. The second most important thing you should make sure you do is to show your son how you want him to act. You can't expect him to be honest with you if you are always lying. The same is true if you bad mouth women around him. He will think that's okay and do the same. In the end, you are his parent, and you know him better than anybody.

Finally, if you found this book useful in any way, a review on Amazon is always appreciated!

Printed in Great Britain
by Amazon

41251437R00091